BELL TRACE

The Older the Fiddle, the Better the Tune

The Older the Fiddle, the Better the Tune

The Joys of Reaching a Certain Age

Willard Scott
and Friends

NEW YORK

Excerpt on pages 97–98 from *Time Flies* by Bill Cosby © 1987 by William H. Cosby Jr. Published by Doubleday, a division of Random House, Inc. Reprinted with permission.

Excerpt on pages 175–76 from *A Ned Rorem Reader* by Ned Rorem © 2001 by Ned Rorem. Published by Yale University Press. Reprinted with permission of the author.

LIBRARY OF CONGRESS CATALOGING-IN-PUBLICATION DATA

Scott, Willard.
    The older the fiddle, the better the tune : the joys of reaching a certain age / Willard Scott and friends.
       p. cm.
    ISBN 0-7868-6892-9
       1. Aged. 2. Aged—Biography. 3. Aged—Conduct of life.
    4. Self-realization in old age. 5. Aging. I. Title.

HQ1061 .S353   2003
305.26—dc21

                                    2002192213

Hyperion books are available for special promotions and premiums. For details contact Hyperion Special Markets, 77 West 66th Street, 11th floor, New York, New York 10023-6298, or call 212-456-0133.

Book design by Richard Oriolo

FIRST EDITION

10 9 8 7 6 5 4 3 2 1

Acknowledgments

A book such as this one is the cumulative effort of many talented and dedicated people. First and foremost, I am forever grateful to Tracy Quinn McLennan, whose research and editing skills guided this book wisely throughout the process. Special thanks to Bill Adler and Mary Nettleton of Bill Adler Books, Inc.; Bill Adler, Jr., and Jeanne Tyrrell Welsh of Adler & Robin Books, Inc.; and Wayne McLennan for their tireless work. Finally, thank you to Jennifer Lang and Will Schwalbe at Hyperion for seeing this book to fruition.

Thank you to the many senior centers, organizations, and interested parties that encouraged the contributors to share their thoughts on the great things about getting older, most notably, Tom Blake, columnist of "Single Again" and author of *Middle Aged and*

Dating Again; the Worldwide Seniors organization; Joyce Dunn, Associate State Director, AARP, North Carolina; Katrina Hayday-Wester, www.iGrandparents.com; Mary Johnson, editor for "The Social Security & Medicare Advisor," TREA Senior Citizens League, www.tscl.org; Judene Edgar, Abbeyfield New Zealand; Mary David, National Secretary-Treasurer, the National Association of Retired & Veteran Railway Employees, Inc. (NARVRE); Bea Mitz, teacher of life history classes at West Hollywood Center, Pico Robertson Center, and Bridgepoint Retirement Home, Los Angeles, California; Chuck Ridgeway, President, Maryland Retired Teachers Association; Betsy Gladish, Activity Director, ATRIA Retirement & Assisted Living, Tucson, Arizona; and Mary K. Creel, Roanoke-Chowan Publications, LLC, Ahoskie, North Carolina.

The age of a woman doesn't mean a thing.
The best tunes are played on the oldest fiddles.
—SIGMUND Z. ENGEL

Introduction

It's true—*The older the fiddle, the better the tune.*
I'm getting better and better at playing the tune, as I've had years of practice! I was born on March 7, 1934, and have worked in the media for more than fifty years. A half a century, I can hardly believe it. In my work, I've been able to meet people of all ages. As the first Ronald McDonald, I met exuberant children who showed a love of life and a curiosity about the world around them. As the weatherman on NBC's *Today* show, I have had the privilege of wishing happy birthday to energetic centenarians, the men and women lucky enough to have made it to the milestone of living 100 years or more.

The two best times of life are arguably childhood

and being older. That may explain why grandparents and grandchildren get along so well—they have so much in common. Both children and grandparents enjoy—and have the time for—play, rest, and wondering about the world.

I have had a wonderful life—terrific jobs, a loving family, and the opportunity to meet many amazing people. I am happy to be enjoying a fulfilling and satisfactory age, but I wondered recently if others were as lucky as I am. So I decided to survey some people and ask them all the same question: What are the great things about getting older, and do you have any advice to the younger generations on how best to enjoy their years? You'll recognize many of the names of the people in this collection from the worlds of entertainment, sports, government, publishing, and fashion, among others. Many of the names will be unfamiliar to you, but their responses will seem like something you've already heard, perhaps a conclusion you've already come to on your own, or an element of growing older to look forward to.

The consensus was that getting older *is* great for many reasons: You have more wisdom, memories, experience, free time, a gentler-paced life, and grandchildren—especially grandchildren. Lee R. Brobst, who is eighty-three years old, says, "Because the burdens of youth, earning a living, and gaining experience are now history, there is time to reflect upon and savor the memories of the then unrealized pleasures that were associated with those years."

And contrary to popular wisdom, time doesn't speed up as you get older. As the contributors to this book aptly show, time actually slows down in the most magnificent and majestic ways. The hectic, frenzied, almost overwhelming velocity of life that's part of the "younger years" is over. Your time becomes your own—not your children's or your employer's. Gone are the days when you are too busy to smell the roses, thumb through your photo album, enjoy a game of tennis, take a swim when you feel like it, or write in your journal. Charlotte Nedell, who is 100 years old, says that she was too busy working and raising a family in her younger years to have time to enjoy nature and now loves to "pause, relax and look up at the sky, and appreciate the beauty."

Of course, getting older doesn't necessarily mean people are no longer active. Joan Grindley published her first book in her late sixties. Charles W. Wittman began college at age sixty-nine, and Betty Perkins-Carpenter is studying for her doctorate at age seventy-one. Stan Wallace, who is eighty-eight, finds joy in using his computer. Edith H. Aschenbach, who is 100 years old, took up painting when she was seventy. Many other seniors find fulfillment in volunteering, like Bobbie Yankovich, who in her seventies volunteers as a Chemo Angel for patients undergoing treatment for cancer, and says, "There is no end to what you can do when you do not have to worry about going to work every day." Jack Burgeman and Ruth H. Iliff find working in museums a way to share their knowledge with others and meet interesting people. Bob and Audrey Nelsen bought a fifth-wheel trailer and visited forty-eight states in fifteen years. Joseph S. Colletto enjoys sailing his two tugboats off the western shore of the United States. And last year, at the age of eighty-one, Janet Quirk traveled solo, 8,383 miles, from Maine around the entire country, returning home more than a month later.

The rewards of reaching a certain age are many. Yogi Berra says, "You don't have to take any guff from anyone," and Darcy Lewis says, "You can get away with being feisty." Art Linkletter wisely points out that "the things you buy now will never wear out." And John Updike finds that "one of the joys of being over sixty-five is that people have stopped trying to sell you life insurance." Ruthe Williams says that she is pleased to have reached an age when her experiences allow her to share wisdom with so many younger people. Jack Leroy Bryson adds, "At seventy years of age one great thing is that I still have as much to look forward to as I can look back on." Art

Buchwald says, "The great thing about getting older is that you can pretend you do not hear someone that you don't want to hear." And Lorene M. Chiancola is a testament that finding love—even your *first* love all over again—happens even when you're a senior.

I hope you enjoy reading this collection, but more important, I hope that the sound of your tune continues to get better and better, as you do.

—WILLARD SCOTT
October 2002

I have always felt that I look younger than I am when looking into a mirror. This attitude has made me wonder why my friends are looking older. I believe that a full and active life contributes to this logic. Of course, having been in space for almost three hundred hours has made me 1.5 seconds less old than you earthlings.

—**WALLY SCHIRRA,** born March 12, 1923, was one of the original seven astronauts and the only astronaut to have flown on all three spacecraft—*Mercury, Gemini,* and *Apollo*; as command pilot, he flew the initial flight of the Apollo series, *Apollo 7.*

*H*ere's some philosophy I would like to pass on to other seniors (and everyone else). I was very fortunate to have a dad who taught me that anyone can do whatever they want to do *and be good at it* if they set their mind to it. People are like fruit. We grow so long as we are green. As soon as we think we are ripe, that's when we start to get rotten.

—**MURRAY STEIN,** born March 22, 1927, is a retired electronics engineer who also pursued an art career in exotic sculpture and worked in the private sector on a project that resulted in the simulator design for the Apollo mission.

∾

*W*hile I thoroughly enjoyed my working years, I long looked forward to retirement by the tender age of sixty. I had my own business, which employed forty people, and found myself working seven days a week, many days from six in the morning until nine at night, with just enough time for a quick sandwich. As I approached my goal of retiring at sixty, I was fortunate enough to find a buyer for my company who would take good care of my customers. So I sold it for enough money to enjoy my golden years.

Ten years later, I opted to move to a wonderful retirement community in sunny Fort Myers, Florida. No more snow, no more household chores, and best of all, plenty of time to relax and do what I wanted to do when I wanted. After two weeks of sitting on my eighth-floor porch watching the boats up and down the Caloosahatchee River, I got bored and decided to do some volunteer work—something that I would enjoy doing. I joined the retirement community model railroad club to do the electrical work. Then I designed and installed a surround sound for our ballroom so that residents could see recent movies on Saturday night in a home theater setting. Shortly after, I discovered that the system provided excellent sound for classical music CDs, so there went my Sundays. Not satisfied with enough to do, I learned to play the recorder, and joined a group that puts on concerts several times a year. Then I was elected to represent the residents in our building to help them resolve issues that come up with management. So, there went my days of boat watching on the Caloosahatchee River.

What started off to be relaxing days where nothing ever had to be done, again ended up with a busy schedule of activities from dawn to dusk, seven days a week. But, do you know what? I have never had so much fun and made so many new friends. Not only have I had an opportunity to make a better life for others, but I feel twenty years younger.

—**CHUCK DURRELL,** born July 23, 1927, is a retired electrical engineer and small-business owner.

> If wrinkles must be written upon our brows,
> let them not be written upon the heart.
> The spirit should not grow old.
>
> —JAMES A. GARFIELD

I wonder if that quality of *appreciation* isn't one of the things that "older" people learn to specialize in. I know that the older I get, the more I seem to be able to appreciate my "neighbor" (whomever I happen to be with at the moment). Oh, sure, I've always tried to love my neighbor as myself; however, the more experiences I've had, the more chances I've had to see the uniqueness of each person—as well as each tree, and plant, and every day in the lavish gifts of God, who I've come to believe is the greatest appreciator of all.

—FRED ROGERS, born March 20, 1928, is the host of *Mister Rogers' Neighborhood* and the recipient of many awards, including Emmys and the Presidential Medal of Freedom.

I am now approaching my seventy-eighth birthday. I do not feel that age, and I constantly wonder where the years have gone. It is so important for everyone to appreciate how quickly time passes and make certain they do not put off doing the things they want to do before the passage of time makes it impossible.

The advice I give to young people, when I am asked, is: Make sure you are happy with your chosen occupation. If you find that you are not, then take immediate measures to change your situation. Your workday is one-third of your life, and if you are not happy with what you are doing, it will adversely impact on your nonworking hours as well.

So, no matter how much time, effort, and money you have put into achieving the status you have, if you are not happy after a reasonable amount of time, stop and change your situation.

—**EDWARD I. KOCH,** born December 12, 1924, served three terms as mayor of New York City from 1978 to 1989.

~

O ne of the nicest benefits of getting older is the fact that grandkids and great-grandkids can be enjoyed to their *very fullest* and then they go home. At eighty, I feel the generation gap at last; these children are too smart, but isn't that great! I find the great-grands keep my vocabulary updated. Blessed are the grannies who live to see these little wonders and to make a nice contribution to their lives.

—**BARBARA BRAUN**, born September 5, 1922, worked for the U.S. Naval Supply, Department of Defense, then for community services; she has six children, thirteen grandchildren, and ten great-grandchildren.

∽

*Y*ou know, it's true. Age is a remarkable means of acquiring wisdom, and I would like to offer a little tale that happened to me many years ago.

As a practicing young physician, I was attempting to overcome my youthful appearance when a middle-aged former patient brought her visiting aged mother in to me for a checkup. Her daughter stated she was ninety-two. She was a neat little old lady and obviously in good health. I proceeded to place the blood pressure cuff on her and attempted to make small talk to overcome any possibility of anxiety.

"Tell me, dearie," I went on, "to what do you attribute your longevity?"

She was hard of hearing and didn't respond. I bent over near her ear and repeated the above-mentioned statement.

She turned to me, paused for a moment, and then cackled back, "I stayed away from doctors."

I'm now retired.

After many years of practice, and with the alteration of the physician/patient relationship, not to mention the cost of care, and governmental and private business intervention, I'm not sure the old gal didn't have the wisdom of Solomon.

—DR. ROBERT M. HUNT, born November 24, 1923, was enlisted with the U.S. Navy during World War II and became a doctor of osteopathy after serving, later opening his own practice and becoming medical director of a hospital that he founded; he has been married for fifty-four years and has three children and five grandchildren.

∽

1. The things you buy now will never wear out.

2. You discover that you can get along (even grumpily) without sex, but you absolutely have to have your glasses.

3. In case you are taken hostage by kidnappers in a plane, you will be among the first released.

4. You accept the philosophy that it is better to be over the hill than under it.

5. You admit that money may be the root of all evil, but there is one great soothing rec-

ommendation—it keeps your children in touch with you.

6. And finally I have just celebrated my ninetieth birthday and I find life to be hugely rewarding and filled with memories that are priceless.

—**ART LINKLETTER,** born July 17, 1912, is a television host and author of twenty-three books, including *Kids Say the Darndest Things*, one of the top-selling nonfiction books in history.

∽

"79"

Being 79 is not so bad,
look at all the fun I've had.

I joined the Navy and went off to war,
and was very proud of the uniform I wore.

I came home and married a gal,
who was, also, my best pal.

She gave me children, numbering three,
adding to our family tree.

Now we have grandchildren, I'm happy to say,
also great-grandchildren showing us the way.

Next year I'll be 80, God willing,
and life will be more filling.

Our next goal in this great game,
is to be in Willard Scott's Hall of Fame.
. . . 100

—CHARLES W. McCLELLAND, born October 16,
1923, is a former member of the U.S. Navy and a retired
draftsman.

∾

We were at an elder hostel in Sydney, Australia. One morning while standing in line waiting for the museum to open, I overheard a conversation by two elementary schoolchildren in the line next to ours. One asked, "Who are all those old people in the next line?" The other answered, "Oh, those are a bunch of elder fossils."

—MAURICE BENDER, born July 22, 1918, is retired
from the U.S. Public Health Service.

∾

I have never understood why the majority of people have a fear of getting older, because there are so many wonderful and fun things associated with maturity. For instance . . .

By a certain age . . .

One learns that to give in to the petty annoyances of life is just an unnecessary emotional expenditure. As the old cliché states: "Most of the things we worry about never happen."

By a certain age . . .

We can generally state what is on our minds without fear of censorship, because the younger generation will come to the conclusion that we have either developed into a delightfully quaint "character" or just reached an acceptable and harmless stage of senility. Unbeknownst to them and much to our mature amusement, we consider either judgment a win-win proposition.

By a certain age . . .

When we are told that it is time to retire from our profession, we find, to our delight, that there is no expiration date on our creativity or enthusiasm for life and that now we have time to explore both to our hearts' content.

By a certain age . . .

We can indulge our grandchildren in things we would never have allowed our children to do.

By a certain age . . .

We can all return to the perks of childhood, like spending a day at Disneyland, wearing sport clothes during the week, eating cotton candy or ice cream and not worrying if we get stains on our shirt or blouse, and learning new things every day that we never knew before.

And best of all ... by a certain age ...

We can look at our adult children with pride and know that we did a good job of bringing them up to be the responsible and compassionate kind of people that help to make our world a little bit better just for them being in it.

—**SYBIL JASON,** born November 23, 1929, was a child actress in 1930s American films.

∿

*A*ll I can say is I am glad I am as old as I am. Both my husband and I are in our seventies. Mike retired from the space program in 1990 and we have been having fun ever since. We have a motor home and have done a lot of traveling. With our travels we have worked for Habitat for Humanity helping to build houses all over the country. I have also worked in a Salvation Army Thrift Store as a volunteer. We have volunteered at a county park in California. Everything we do now is as a volunteer. Mike has worked at a learning center in Yuma, Arizona, doing building, etc. I volunteer at our library and at our church, and help with serving dinners for the homeless at Thanksgiving. There is no end to what you can do when you do not have to worry about going to work every day.

The best volunteering I do is being a Chemo Angel. It is an organization of over 2,000 angels. We adopt a person that is going through cancer treatment and we send cards and gifts every week as long as we are needed. It is so rewarding, I cannot even explain the feeling I get from doing it.

So you see, getting older can be pretty wonderful.

—**BOBBIE,** born April 8, 1931, is a homemaker, wife, and mother of five children, and **MIKE YANKOVICH,** born November 9, 1928, is a retired engineer for the space program; they have been married for fifty years.

∾

O ne of the great things about getting older is my participation in a senior singing group called the Pavilionaires. After rehearsing for weeks, the director works up a program that we present at nursing homes. The residents of the nursing homes enjoy listening to us and participating in sing-alongs. For one who has an average voice but enjoys singing, this group fits my needs. I've always wanted to sing in a group, but it took my senior years to find an outlet. My husband is also in the group, so this is a togetherness activity for us. My advice to pass on to other generations is to do "togetherness" activities together instead of going your own ways.

—**RUTH B. GLASS,** born November 8, 1928, is a retired schoolteacher.

> No one goes before his time—unless
> the boss leaves early.
> —GROUCHO MARX

*G*rowing older is not that great. But true to the
Emersonian doctrine of "for every gain there is
a loss and for every loss there is a gain," there are
assets to be had as well as frustrations.

What I learned as I have grown older is the in-
creasing reliance I place on my instincts, my intuition, my judgments, when the future can only be
dimly seen, if seen at all. I have grown to trust my
instincts. When a problem arises, others fuss about
it with logic, research, lawyerly searches, and the
like. But I "smell" it and "feel" it because I always
turn to that little elf who lives somewhere between
my belly and my brain, and I listen to that little elf
because his name is "instinct."

I do believe that the longer one lives, the more
sensitive becomes "instinct." I have found over the
years that I am right far more often than I am wrong
at peering through a vapory veil that curtains over
the future. I remember an old friend of mine, the
late Clark Clifford, when asked how he became suc-

cessful. His answer was "making the right decisions" and when queried on how to make right decisions, he answered, "by making wrong decisions." Pretty apt, and accurate.

The other thing I have learned is that if one keeps fit—and I mean really fit—one can extend active life much longer than the catalog of the calendar so sourly prescribes. Older life can bring much delight in doing that which older people are not supposed to be able to do physically. But keeping fit means religiously exercising every day. Somehow, I find the time to do that, as one goes to church, knowing that absence may bring down upon you the wrath of the Higher Being who inhabits that church.

Finally, always have fun doing whatever you do. If it isn't fun, stop doing it. So when you bring them all together, following your instincts honed by experience, keeping fit and having fun doing your daily chores, you can find the older years not that unsuitable. Well, it would be better to be younger, but what the hell, you have no choice, since time hits us all with the same velocity.

—**JACK VALENTI**, born September 5, 1921, is Chairman and Chief Executive Officer of the Motion Picture Association of America.

∽

I am eighty-seven years old. Even though I went through my most devastating time with the death of my husband, whom I dearly loved, I have the opportunity and ability now to appreciate a new and different experience: living without my husband of sixty-three years.

As a child, I remember overhearing my parents describe me as self-willed and determined. I guess I was self-motivated, because I decided early on to be prepared to meet the challenges that life offered.

In 1932, at seventeen, I made a decision to attend college in the mornings and help my father, a second-generation wholesale New York furrier, in the afternoons. I wanted to learn all aspects of his business in order to keep the family's fur business tradition alive. During those years, I learned the difference between good and bad skins, how the manufacturing process works, and the fine points of selling.

After my father died, I decided to leave the wholesale market because it was dirty and women were considered easy sexual prey. So at the age of forty-five, I decided to take my expertise to the retail market.

Little did I know that fine New York retail stores did not hire women over forty-five, regardless of experience. I heard that Saks Fifth Avenue needed a man to run their men's fur department. I decided that job was for me! I was interviewed by the manager, the buyer, and the president of the fur department. They were impressed with my résumé but wanted a man. On my own, I went to see the president of Saks Fifth Avenue. Much to my surprise, I got an appointment. I promised him that under my management, with my experience, his store would be the talk of the town. I think he was stunned, but he said he'd let me know. The following morning his office called: The job was mine. And I did a bang-up job. Our figures were astronomical and people came from all over the world to buy men's furs in "my" department.

Years later, when my husband decided to retire in Honolulu, where our son was a practicing physician, I decided to open a fur salon in a prestigious women's ready-to-wear store. When I told people my plans, they laughed. "Furs in Honolulu, that's funny. It's hot as hell there." But I did it, and successfully, too. I always thought that once a person hit fifty, he/she was over the hill. Not so in Honolulu; age was revered there. That was lucky for me, as I moved there when I was fifty-nine and was still considered young. I'm glad about that, for I continued working until I was eighty-one.

As I aged, I learned to respect myself for being able to direct my skills into good positions in which I found success professionally and financially. If I knew then what I know now, I could have been a less demanding person and still been successful.

Old age is a wonderful time for reflection of life's ups and downs, its pains as well as successes. Viva old age!

—**MARIAN REICH,** born December 17, 1914, has been active in her family's fur business and worked in New York in the wholesale fur trade and later as head of Saks Fifth Avenue's men's fur department; she has one son.

∽

*Y*ou don't have to take any guff from anyone. If you don't really want to do something, you don't have to. Unless your wife says it's real important.

—**YOGI BERRA,** born May 12, 1925, was one of baseball's greatest catchers and the manager of the New York Yankees and the New York Mets.

∽

I am having the time of my life right now.

No, I'm not going to wild parties or traveling to exotic places. That never was my "thing." I am living in the home that Anne and I built eighteen years ago, close to my family, friends, and church, and I have a feeling of contentment and being right with the world. I do not want to be young again. I have no desire to make all those mistakes again and reexperience the "growth" period of my life. Some

think that if they had their life to live over, they would avoid the mistakes. But there would be others in their place. Besides, I would not want to change anything, because to do so would change the outcome, and my life would not be the same.

Anne and I were gifted with three children whose marriage partners have become as our children. We were further gifted with nine grandchildren, our legacy and our pride.

During much of my working years, I had many doubts about God and religion. I was immersed in my work almost to the exclusion of everything and everyone else, and I tried to convince everyone, including myself, that it was for my family. I loved my work.

During the years that our children were growing up, Anne kept our focus on them. She stayed at home and raised them while I worked two jobs or extra hours. Our travels were limited to short trips to the boys' baseball tournaments. Of traveling, Anne said that if she didn't have it at least as good as at home, it was no vacation. Our funds went into making our home into the place where we wanted to be. Later we took a few vacations and we enjoyed the company's annual management meetings in Tucson, Palm Springs, or similar places. During these trips we enjoyed "living in the manner to which we would like to become accustomed," a favorite saying of a former president of the company.

By the time I retired, our home was our personal retirement resort. Anne and I had both discovered that spirituality was not a far-off supernatural thing but an integral part of human life. We both became very active in our church. After five years of retirement and a few days before a planned trip for our forty-fifth anniversary, Anne succumbed to a sudden heart attack. This was fourteen years after her first heart attack and bypass surgery. Anne and I often thanked God for these wonderful years.

I now realize I had been well prepared for her loss. We had often joked about "who would go first," and we were both content that our lives had been good and fruitful. Because of Anne's health problems, including the side effects of diabetes, I had been in training, helping with the laundry and other things. We had started using a cleaning service every other week and I have continued that along with a lawn maintenance service. So, after Anne's death, when a neighbor asked if I was going to put the house up for sale, I replied, "No, my kids are going to do that after they carry me out."

In addition to being very active in lay ministry at church, I had started a website for the parish. It is something I enjoy and it is a worthwhile hobby. I spend several hours a week updating that website.

After Anne's death I realized that there were many things that my grandchildren, and others, did not know about us. I also felt that I had things of value that I wanted to tell them. I started a website of my own. The site, "The World of Grandpa Don," has become a weekly newsletter, a family history, and a place where I encourage my grandchildren by recording their accomplishments. It contains my thoughts and beliefs and is, I hope, a witness to the actions of God in our lives.

My purpose in life at this time is to assist my children and their families when I can, in any way I can. It is to present a positive example to my grandchildren and to encourage them to live with love, kindness, and concern for their fellow man. I try to pass on my belief that we should not just show tolerance to those who differ from us; we should embrace the differences, and benefit from them. That, in my opinion, is what made the U.S.A. a successful nation. I hope that they will continue to learn that when you compete, you should compete with yourself in an effort to better yourself, but not at the expense of others. There is no need to diminish someone to build yourself. It is more productive to bring others up with you, thereby raising the level for all. My message to my grandchildren is to use their God-given talents to the benefit of all God's creation. We are not isolated individuals but part of a world community dependent on the abilities of one another. I encourage all, in relationships with others, to "be nicer than you need to be." These messages are there for any who visit my web pages.

Anne is no longer here and our parents are gone, as are many relatives and friends. I miss them, but I celebrate having them as part of my life. I love my life, past and present, and have no fear of the future. I am having the time of my life right now endeavoring to show kindness to everyone I meet. I hope it is contagious.

—**DONALD J. PLEFKA,** born May 6, 1931, is a retired vice president of an electrical contracting company.

∾

*G*etting older is an honor. It allows you to spend time with old friends, have reunions, enjoy a long and beautiful marriage (fifty-five years) with your wife, watch your children grow into successful citizens, and best of all, experience the joy of grandchildren. My advice to younger generations? Think like forty when you are eighty—and act that way.

—**MONTY HALL,** born August 25, 1921, emceed daytime game shows such as *What's This Song?, P.D.Q.,* and *Let's Make a Deal.*

∾

I have just purchased a second twenty-six-foot Nordic Tug, one for San Francisco Bay, my home, and one for Puget Sound and cruising the

Northwest. I am a longtime solo-sailor, and still do most of my boating solo, as at my age, seventy-six, most of my longtime friends are interested in other things than bouncing around on the water. In searching for a name for the new Tug, one thing I kept hearing was "Two tugboats...? We wonder if Old Joe is losing it." There was so much wonderment, I decided that I would incorporate it into the new name, and it became *Wee Wonder,* an appropriate name for a twenty-six-foot tugboat and for those who are still wondering. If you see me cruising in the Northwest in *Wee Wonder* or in *Little Toot* in San Francisco Bay, give me a wave—I'll be enjoying my son's inheritance.

—**JOSEPH S. COLLETTO,** born May 27, 1926, had his own franchise and sold heavy equipment and later worked in real estate.

∾

"Courage at Seventy"

Now it is certain
There is no magic stone
No secret to be found,

One must go
With the mind's
Winnowed learning

No more than a child's handhold
On willows bending over the lake
On sumac roots at the cliff edge

Ignorance is checked
Betrayals scratched
The coat has been hung on the peg.

The cigar laid on the table edge
The cue chosen and chalked
The balls racked for the final break.

The dice warm as blood in the palm
Shaken for the last cast
The glove has been thrown to the ground

The last choice of weapons made

A book for one thought
A poem for one line
A line for one word

Broken things are powerful
Things about to break are stronger still
The last shot from the brittle bow

Is the truest.

—E. J. (EUGENE) McCARTHY, born March 29, 1916, ran for the 1968 Democratic presidential nomination and was a member of the U.S. Congress from Minnesota as a representative from 1949 to 1959 and a senator from 1959 to 1971.

~

There are many stages to one's life. As a youth, one can't wait until old enough to get a driver's license. When in school, one can't wait until finished to begin a life of one's own. When a teenager, one can't wait to get out from under parents' discipline and be free to make a life independent from others. At midlife we begin to fear old age. After retirement we wonder why we had all those concerns.

In reality age is relative. The perspective changes as the years go by. Now at age eighty-three, there is a tendency to look back and regret not having capitalized better on the many opportunities that came along over those eighty-three years. Yet, from this perspective, I now also realize how fortunate I have been and am now thankful for all the wonderful things that came my way.

Among the joys of living at this age is the wealth of knowledge I have accumulated. I was fortunate to have been exposed to many and varied situations that at the time challenged my capability, but at the same time added to my ability to make better judgments. Some of this came from my parents' teaching, some from schooling, but the best came from experience. It is pleasurable to pass this wealth of knowledge on to the younger generation, even though I sometimes wonder if they comprehend the importance of just listening. Yet, when I see them eventually grasp a bit of that wisdom and use it productively, it is a reward and a pleasure unattainable elsewhere.

One of the greatest joys at this age is the friends that surround me—my wife, our son and family, the grandchildren and great-grandchildren, and those whom I met during my working career, fraternities, and otherwise. Because the burdens of youth, earning a living, and gaining experience are now history, there is time to reflect upon and savor the memories of the then unrealized pleasures that were associated with those years. Life has been good to me and my perspective has changed. I can look back and truthfully say, "Well done, thou good and faithful servant," and feel confident that I have prepared well for life after death and the eternity that is waiting.

—**LEE R. BROBST,** born April 23, 1919, worked as a finance officer in the Cooperative Farm Credit System and later chief of staff to the senior deputy governor of the Farm Credit Administration.

∾

I was talking with someone in officialdom recently—I need a good reason for divulging any personal data—when she asked, "And what is your birthdate?" "2-11-19," I said. There was a short, reflective pause, then, with a slight irritation in her voice, she said, "19 what?"

—**LILLIAN LUBIN KRELOVE,** born February 11, 1919, worked half of her life as a horticulturist and garden writer and the other half as a bookseller and publisher of folklore books.

∿

*T*here are five great things about getting older, which I am going to list in a moment. There is nothing wrong, ever, with being older or getting older. There is always something wrong with being sick or alone or broke or injured or discriminated against; and these conditions are even worse for people of advanced age.

Our culture has developed the weird habit of putting age into the same basket as impairment and decrepitude. The proper attitude should be the reverse. The older a person gets, the more of a triumph that person is against the forces that try to pull us down, in our cribs, in midlife and in old age. An old person, simply by virtue of accumulated years, is a victory over these forces.

Naturally, the longer you live, the more chance

you have of running afoul of some disease or disorder. (If you cross a busy street a hundred times, you are more likely to be hit by a truck than if you cross it ten times.) And we are not physically immortal. We are eventually overtaken by entropy, even if we never get cancer or heart disease or kidney failure or Alzheimer's. But once we accept this fact, and if we are wise enough to modify risks and lucky enough to avoid the conditions listed in the first paragraph, we will find some magnificent advantages to getting old.

First, assuming you have gotten your act together at least by middle age, you will have developed techniques for coping that can make life an easy and pleasant journey. You are in command of your comfort—something a young person does not have. (A young person can enjoy comfort, or feelings of satisfaction, but only as fate or chance dole them out— the young person cannot create them.)

Second, you gain control of sex. When you are young, sex has control of you, and this can lead to considerable suffering. Sex, like fire, is a wonderful servant but a terrible master.

Third, in youth, there is a shrouded future at your arm. You don't know you'll make it to seventy, or live through a war and have grandchildren, or be successful in a chosen occupation. I know I will make it to seventy because I did—eleven years ago.

I know I won't be killed in World War II because I went into and came out of the army without a scratch. I know my children and grandchildren, and that my family is not going to be dysfunctional. This kind of knowledge is a source of enormous gratification, and is not available to the young. (It also generates a lot of gratitude, which is itself a pleasant emotion.)

Fourth, successful projects can be enjoyed by older people three times—in three separate phases: (1) Anticipation and planning, (2) the actual accomplishing, and (3) savoring in memory what was accomplished. Young people, having difficulty with deferring gratification, find little enjoyment in accomplishment until it is accomplished, and then seldom savor the reward in retrospect because they feel they should always "look ahead" and never back. Wrong! You can have it three ways, when you're older.

Fifth, a genuine, noticeable increase in quality living comes with age. The majestic wheel of the day takes on a beauty that you took for granted in the hectic heat of young and prime years. The young are too busy to enjoy, too driven by the fires of ambition and sex, too lost in dreams and hopes to have fulfillment and certainty, and too loosely wrapped to develop and fine-tune an esthetic sense that finds beauty in every vista, every meal, every drink, every well-written book, and every bar of good music. These come with age.

The poet Robert Browning wrote: "Grow old along with me! The best is yet to be," a sentence I thought was errant nonsense when I first read it. But I was young. And I was wrong.

Browning was right.

—HUGH DOWNS, born February 14, 1921, is a journalist who coanchored *20/20*, hosted the *Today* show, and helped launch *The Tonight Show*.

∾

I have had a dream to be a writer since I was old enough to hold a pencil. The greatest reward for me in growing older was to finally have an opportunity to pursue that dream. Years of raising a family were followed by divorce and the necessity to forge a career for myself—a career that did not include writing, unfortunately. The one good thing that came out of the divorce was that it forced me to start writing again in my spare time. I was devastated by the death of my marriage but could not afford professional help, so I turned to writing as a form of therapy. By putting down my thoughts and feelings, I was encouraging myself to heal.

When I retired from my career at sixty-six, I could not wait to begin writing again. I had the advantage of now being computer literate and so began immediately with a computer of my own. I was spurred on by a promise I had made to my maternal grandmother, who lived an amazing life and with whom I spent childhood summers. At her death she extracted this promise from me to write her story. I have spent the last three years of my life doing just that. *Julia* became a reality last month when it was finally published by Xlibris.

Now in my seventieth year I am hard at work on my second novel, which, strangely enough, is based on those musings and thoughts written down so long ago following my divorce. You have only to have experienced life for these past seventy years to know how exciting and meaningful life really is. How easy it is to follow your dream if only you have enough faith in yourself to persist.

—**JOAN GRINDLEY,** born May 30, 1932, was a corporate executive in community relations until her retirement and is now a writer.

Those who love deeply never grow old; they may die of old age, but they die young.

—BENJAMIN FRANKLIN

I was chatting with my husband, David Brown, this morning about what are some of the great things about getting older—letter request from my friend Willard Scott. "David," I said, "there *aren't* any. Everything gets *worse*! [I'm eighty; David is eighty-six.] There is that arthritic shoulder, one-twelfth the energy you had only ten years ago, you can remember what you ate at a high school banquet but not what you had for breakfast yesterday morning," etc. David said, "Would you rather have stopped everything about age fifty-five and just not experienced any of the *good* things that happened to you the past twenty-five years?" "No, David," I said, "that isn't what I had in mind." I guess I'll just have to accept how old I am, be grateful for the *good* stuff, but not try to be all that excited about *now*. I know I'm going to have to shut up and not tell the next young woman who offers me a seat on the bus (a man is okay) to *shove* it. I don't want her thinking I look like somebody who needs to sit down. As for wisdom to pass on to younger generations, I could only suggest what I tell *any* generation that asks: Whether it's work, household, or social, do the crummy stuff first every day, save the best for last. Life works better that way.

—**HELEN GURLEY BROWN,** born February 18, 1922, is the author of the book *Sex and the Single Girl* and six others as well as a newspaper column, "Woman Alone." She was the editor of *Cosmopolitan* magazine from 1965 to 1996.

$\sim$

*A*ll throughout my life, I wanted to be older. When I was sixteen, I wanted to be twenty-five, and at age twenty-five, I wanted to be fifty so that I could retire. Then at age fifty, I wanted to be sixty-five so that I could get all the senior discounts. But it all happened so fast, and now I want it to stop. Now it seems time is going by so fast, I feel like I may have missed something.

Where has all the time gone? Not long ago, I could ride the bus to New York for just three cents and buy an ice-cream cone for five cents.

During those days, my brother and I would travel south every year, looking for work in the fields. At the end of the week, we would be paid fifty cents and the first thing we would do was head into town and buy ice cream. Those were good times.

When I was twelve years old, cigarettes cost twelve cents. Of course, this was back in the fifties, back when kids used to play "Johnny on the Pony," hide-and-seek, post office, and all sorts of games.

You don't see that sort of thing anymore. Yep, those were the good old days, back when I was a working man and time used to go by so slow. Now it's *Vep, Vam, Voom*, and then before you know it, the week is gone. I used to think there were no days like the "good old days."

I like the way I am living now. I have come into quite a bit: a good wife, a house, a car, a truck, a boat, and all the good food I could ever eat.

My wife, I met some thirty years ago, and now she is my best friend, my lover, and my girlfriend.

Come to think of it, as a senior, these really are the good old days, and that's the way I like it.

—LIVINGSTON WARD, born March 26, 1937, is a retired New York City bus operator.

∽

I'm seventy-six years old and in dog years that's a lot of years, but I feel as young today as I ever did. More so now because I have more time to enjoy *life!*

I'm still active in my profession and will never retire. I hope we will be around together for you to announce my 100th birthday.

For me, life got *more* exciting after fifty!

—KAYE BALLARD, born November 20, 1926, performed on the vaudeville circuit, on the Broadway stage, and in television and films.

∽

*T*he life of a senior citizen can be very rewarding. At this time of your life, your time is all your own and you can do whatever you want with it. You can plan your day to be useful for yourself or for others, and it is very satisfying to know whatever you do to extend yourself will make you feel better.

If you are feeling well enough to be independent, you can take care of yourself and run errands such as shopping, keeping medical appointments, attending church, and taking part in the morning or evening service.

You can also spend time reading books of your choice, keep your house clean, do the laundry, and keep yourself looking good. Sometimes, it's good to spend your time leisurely, just lying back and doing nothing, without feeling the slightest bit guilty.

It's a great time to be thankful, after experiencing life through the fifties, the sixties, seventies, and on into the twenty-first century. Besides, it just feels good still being able to be free and just be "me."

—IDA McFEETERS, born March 18, 1927, was a registered nurse.

~

I had been active all my life making things happen. I have enjoyed working with others to save a river, to open doors to wider horizons for women, to create a spay and neuter clinic for animals, etc. I had received many awards and much recognition. I felt that I had had such a rich and full life that I now could be content to stay home to enjoy my maturing family, my large garden and fruit orchard I had planted. I had had my "last hurrah."

However, it occurred to me that at seventy-five I still could expect another twenty-five years of life. At twenty-five the next twenty-five years were full of life, love, children. At fifty, the next twenty-five years included two college degrees, many civic successes, independence, and two husbands, one of which I still have.

So at seventy-five with twenty-five years to go, I realized that of course I could still do a lot of things. So I got busy.

I was able to help a young Native American author self-publish his first book, 600 copies already sold. I was elected to public office and am now running unopposed for a second term. There are many deserving people out there who need a little help over a rough spot. I like to help them anonymously. If they find out, the help stops. That is my hobby. So many people have helped me along my life's way. I love it that now I can help some others without hearing declarations of gratitude.

However, the big change came to me when I realized I had so many years left. Those who expect to live a long time do live the longest because they plan for it. Now I tell everyone I can reach, no matter their age, to decide how long they are going to live. It makes such a difference in the way they will live their life. You have heard that remark, "If I had known I was going to live this long, I would have taken better care of myself." Plan on it. You will be glad you did.

—RUTH ANDERSON WILSON, born January 31, 1923, is a retired property manager and is a professional civic volunteer.

∾

They used to call old age your "declining years"; not true anymore. I am enjoying eighty-five and whatever follows so much, I've changed the old saw from Golden Years to Platinum Years. People tell you, "You look great," no matter how you look. They help you up and down stairs. If you say you can't stand the draft, they'll close the window and sit in a sweat. In other words, you are treated with kindness and respect. Isn't it glorious!

—PHYLLIS DILLER, born July 17, 1917, is considered the first woman stand-up comic.

∾

*M*y goal in life is to play golf when I am ninety-two. I am not a good golfer, but a fun golfer. Never use the golf cart except to get to the course. Then walk it. Besides golf I love to volunteer, helping others. I won the National AARP award for volunteering a couple of years ago; they called it Aging Gracefully. Had a huge banquet and all the trimmings. I always remember a card my daughter sent me for Mother's Day one year. It said: "Those who dearly love to give, find every day a joy to live." That says it all.

—**THELMA B. HOFFMAN,** born June 5, 1922, was an office manager of an insurance agency and now is an office manager of a community fund.

∽

*S*ince my retirement I have been able to enjoy life much more and appreciate the wonderful things that God has given us and put on this earth that are free—the sunset, the sunrise, watching and enjoying the rain, appreciating spring, and watching nature beautify the earth with everything coming alive again. Flowers blooming, trees, plants, and the grass turn green again. The birds fill the air with happiness, building nests, reproducing their young and suddenly seeing young, baby rabbits running around along with other animals. All these things that I have mentioned are just a few that while we were working we all seem to have taken for granted and never took the time to stop and see and enjoy the wonders of the world that God has given to us.

—**A. JAMES GEMIGNANI,** born November 10, 1921, worked as a district manager of the Illinois Quad City Market with the Joyce Seven Up Company for twenty-five years, then in the same position with the Prudential Insurance Company for fifteen years before retiring.

∽

"Reflections on Turning 80"

They've told the whole wide world how old I am,
And now I'm caught in something of a jam.
I can't believe the way Fate sometimes tricks me!
'Cause now I can't pretend I'm only sixty.
But life is good, I think I'll stick around,
until my mind turns up in Lost and Found
The wisdom that I might have shared with you, is gone,
and frankly, I don't have a clue.
The rest of me is chugging right along,
My engine's in good shape and going strong.
All body parts were here last time I checked;
Some bones and joints are only partly wrecked.
I'm thankful for my family and my friends!
They'll bless my life until the story ends.

So, though I'm eighty, hey, I'm not going yet!
There's still some kick in this old gal, you bet.
And though I haven't found one anywhere,
I keep on looking for that millionaire!

—KATHRYN A. HAMSHAR, born August 18, 1922, worked at a bakery, for Boeing in several aircraft manufacturing divisions, and for a local newspaper; she has three children and has been named Idaho Poet of the Year in 2000 and 2002.

∾

I don't know whether it is a joy or misfortune of old age, but I don't have to worry so much anymore about getting into trouble. I hardly drink, don't smoke, don't gamble, and am kept under very tight control by my wife of forty years. On balance, I think that's an advantage.

As a journalist, I am in a line of work where I can keep working indefinitely. Nobody will even notice when the mind finally gives out. Being an ancient journalist is an advantage for me because I actually covered things that many of my colleagues never even heard of.

The biggest advantage of being hoary, however, is the absence of pressure about what happens to me tomorrow because, obviously, there are many fewer tomorrows. This is an incomparable asset for somebody who issues strong opinions in print and on television. It is really hard to intimidate an old geezer, and that is a delight for me.

—**ROBERT NOVAK,** born February 26, 1931, created the pundit show *The Capital Gang* and is also an occasional cohost on *Crossfire* and interviewer on *Meet the Press.*

∾

*G*rowing older is sometimes living in a smiling world with the grandchildren around. One special time is putting the terra-cotta figures out on the patio. We unwrap each little statue from its winter nest of newspaper. The children decide where it will live for the summer. Rarely does it get a chance to stand where I think it looks good. It is always the site where a child wants to see it so that he can go back to touch it and talk to it again and again.

The fun begins with the question: "What's the story for this one, Oma?" Each figure has a story that I made up, of where it comes from, and why it is living on my patio. The children listen and join in to make the story connect to something they already know. The turtle comes from the river and takes a long time to get here. The chip in the edge of his shell is from crossing a road when a car hit him and rolled him around. The snail has broken his antenna because he is so nosy. He was born out in the woods beside the shagbark hickory tree. The collection of gnomes get names and jobs and find jewels in the rock garden mine just like the seven dwarfs in *Snow White*. One little granddaughter loves to shake her finger and tell them, "Naughty, naughty!" for stepping on the forbidden rocks where children are forbidden to walk. The little angels are thinking about going to McDonald's for hamburgers and ice cream. The chickens and the birds are having a contest to see which one can eat the most bugs. The ducks are protected and cannot be hunted or shot. They have found a place where they know they will be safe under the hosta.

When all of the imagination is finished, the patio doesn't look too bad! There are several places that I will not be able to reach in order to pull out weeds or cut flowers. There are places that I will have to walk around to get to the table to serve lunch. Every year we have a wonderful time and there are lots of memories. I wouldn't change it for all the gold or any manicured garden in the world.

—**VERNA MULDROW**, born December 7, 1932, is a retired teacher and now spends her time writing.

∽

As I inch toward eighty, people keep asking me when I'm going to retire. Why go into hibernation when I'm enjoying what I'm doing so much? Why quit when the creative juices make me jump out of bed each morning ready to go to work? Young people are in such a hurry to experience life, they don't take time to appreciate it. I believe that when you go down the rocky road of life, you should stop and pet a pebble now and then.

Why retire? I leave my kitchen after breakfast every morning, shuffle a few steps to my studio, lie down in my lounge chair 'til I get an idea, shuffle over to my desk to make a few strokes on a piece of paper, and they send me money. What should I retire to . . . ditch digging?

I've been writing and drawing "Beetle Bailey" for over fifty-two years and I still get excited when I get an idea. Over 200 million people read "Beetle" every day, and it pleases me to think how many smiles I bring into the world. I create new characters every five years or so to keep refreshing the interest of the readers. I like to think that I create friends for people who like to start the day by picking up the newspaper and seeing what their old buddy Beetle is doing. Recently I brought in a character who is completely immersed in everything technological. He challenges the old general who can't even program his VCR. And he has challenged me to learn more about computers so that I can write gags for him. It's been very exciting for me and given me a new lease on my career.

Rather than fade away, I feel like my accumulated knowledge and experience is valuable. Cathy and I have a combined family of ten children and twelve grandchildren. They can benefit from what I know but they still can't beat me at golf. Six of our children work with me, writing or drawing or helping in some way. It's fun and rewarding for all of us.

Someone asked me recently how it felt to be getting old. I told them it's sad that so many of my good friends are dead and the ones that are left you can't tell the difference. Luckily I'm in good health and very active. I read the obituaries in the paper every morning and check the ages, then I look at the sun shining and give thanks that it's still shining on me.

I keep getting involved in projects that keep me

hopping. Like starting the International Museum of Cartoon Art, the largest collection of cartoons in the world. As problematic as it has been, it gives me great pleasure to still be contributing to society. Being active like this makes me feel young no matter how old I get.

—**MORT WALKER,** born September 3, 1923, is best known for his creation of the comic strip "Beetle Bailey," which has been running since 1950.

∽

I am seventy-eight. I don't feel a day over seventy-seven. Just kidding.

I am very happy and quite not "very" old.

There are some truly great things about getting older.

When grandkids cry, I can tune out or simply leave.

When a conversation that interests me *not* is, however, engaging to others, I can pretend I don't hear a word. There is danger here, however, because once they think you can't hear, they are apt to say "The old fogy is really out of it now!" Some of our teenagers are more apt to be earthy—not using the word "fogy."

I forget a lot of stuff now, but so what? It is kind of fun to always look for my glasses. (I can now hide my own Easter eggs.)

I always repeat stuff to my kids. Joke telling, however, does have more limitations now. "Dad, you have told us that one a thousand times and it still is not funny."

But my feelings don't get hurt. I just mumble on or totally tune out, sitting back watching all of *them* and counting my own many blessings.

Sometimes I like remembering my own challenges of the past without boring my family about what used to be. Some old guys blow on about how it used to be. I am not even tempted to do that.

It is great being old and having your son be governor of Florida. Having been in politics, I really enjoy watching him work for his state. I hate the campaign rhetoric used to attack him, but my old age and past experience remind me that this just goes with the territory.

And then there is the oldest son. Imagine—father of a president! The only problem with being old is that my pride runneth over and I shed tears too easily when proudly I watch our forty-third president serve his country with pride, dignity, and determination.

And when you are too old, the joy of being about *all* your family is precious. An *abrazo* from a president is very special, but so is a hug from a grandchild.

Being seventy-eight is not bad, not bad at all. Most days it's a privilege.

—GEORGE H. W. BUSH, born June 12, 1924, was the forty-first president of the United States, from 1989 to 1993.

~

In 1944 when I was flying as a navigator in a Flying Fortress over Germany, I knew, as all youngsters did, that I was going to survive. I accepted the fact that people were wounded and some would die. But I would be okay! On my third mission I was scared to death, when one of our engines was hit by flak and caught fire, and we faced the prospect of bailing out over Germany. The engine's fire extinguisher did its job and we all survived. From that day on I knew that death might well come to me and some of my friends.

After every five missions we were given a three-day pass to do anything and go anywhere we wanted to. Strangely enough, that "living 'til the next pass" now became our goal in life. I had learned that I was mortal!

Now at eighty I am probably more mortal than ever, enjoying life as never before, even though each day could be my last. Sure, if I could do it all over, I might do some things differently, but each day is a blessing and I am looking forward to many more great days appreciating my family, friends, the sun and the rain, whatever comes my way. Life as a senior is wonderful.

—**GEORGE C. HOOD,** born May 24, 1922, is a retired corporate personnel director of an aircraft and machinery industry for two international manufacturing companies.

*R*eflecting back over my seventy-eight years, I realize that I have lived with serendipity. Stumbling blocks had become stepping stones to greater wisdom.

Instead of repeating "Woe is me," wake up every morning saying, "What do you have planned for us today, Lord?"—and smile!

—**KAY CARLISI,** born January 7, 1924, is a retired elementary school teacher who also worked in real estate.

~

*G*etting older means having a more than casual acquaintance with strange aches and pains in muscles and joints I never knew I had.

Getting older means having people call me ma'am; even some who I suspect are older than I.

Getting older means finding oneself funnier than anyone else in the world and taking the license to laugh out loud at one's own jokes.

Getting older means having stories to tell on any subject and telling them to anyone who will listen, including one's own self.

Getting older is having the wisdom to know that one really knows very little.

Getting older means having shorter breath, but being long-winded.

Getting older means being able to afford rich

foods which one yearned for in younger days but now finds indigestible.

Getting older means saying good-bye to beloveds too frequently and too painfully.

Yes, to all of the above, but please do what I am going to do—that is, if you have the chance to get older . . . do so.

—**DR. MAYA ANGELOU,** born April 4, 1928, is a poet and author.

$\backsim$

Those who have attained what is usually referred to as "old age" do not usually refer to themselves in that category. Some of us acclaim it with a certain amount of pride, while some of us have nothing complimentary to say about the subject. There are times—when I am rubbing a painful spot with some salve or other—that I have to face facts. Most of the time I consider it a continuation of a happy life.

In contemplating this subject, I believe the most important outlook contains humor. Life is much more acceptable with this ingredient. I don't mean the raucous form of humor. That is acceptable at times, but the basic humorous point of view is easier to live with. I always felt that the choice of a lifemate should include this quality. I was fortunate enough to find one. Basically a serious man, the humor was always lurking in his eyes and ready to be shared. Humor helps us over some trying times. It jars the inclination to look for trouble. Faith in the Almighty is number one on my list. Humor is not far behind.

—**EILEEN CAMPBELL,** born August 24, 1913, is a musician who has been a church organist for sixty years; she has four children, nineteen grandchildren, fourteen great-grandchildren.

∾

*E*ven though I grew up poor and fatherless in the Dust Bowl of the Texas Panhandle during the Depression, I had the advantage of my elders' wisdom as a kid—namely my mother, Ruth Dean, and grandfather Papa Taylor. In fact, I would say that their principles and down-home adages were probably the foundation upon which my life's philosophies were founded.

Mom's mantra was always "We don't take charity, boy, and we don't give up!" after being offered government assistance back then. And as the father figure in my life, Papa Taylor was the wisest man I ever knew; he would always have some bit of wisdom to share, and as a child I would hang on his every word.

After I was older and began performing on national television, Papa Taylor gave me some of the best advice I ever had. He said, "Be yourself, boy, because if people don't like you as you are, they probably won't like you as someone you're trying to be." I've tried never to forget that, whether I was selling a song on stage or a pound of sausage on television. And because of those pearls of wisdom that have guided me through this life, I finally realized that even in the leanest of times, *I may have been broke, but I was never poor.*

I guess one of the good things about getting older is that people will listen to you when you offer advice and wisdom, even if it *is* just out of respect. Now that I'm older and in my mid-seventies, I'd like to think that I've earned a little of that respect, and if the wrinkles come along with it, well, so be it. I don't feel that much different, just a few more aches and pains like everybody else, I guess, though I try hard not to burden other people with them. I'm sure the last thing they want to hear is that my lower back went out again, and how long it took me to put on my britches this morning.

I just hope I never end up like those three old men in the nursing home who were discussing their health problems. Exasperated, one of the old men said, "You know, it's just urinating that's my biggest problem ... mine is one of those start and stop propositions. It'd be so nice if I could just go a good full stream." Another said, "Well, that doesn't bother me at all ... my problem is doing number two. If I just didn't have to take all those danged laxatives." Finally, the third old man chimed in, "Well, boys . . . neither one of those bothers me. Every morning at seven-thirty I do number one just like that . . . at eight o'clock I do a healthy number two. My problem is that I don't wake up until nine-thirty!"

—**JIMMY DEAN,** born August 10, 1928, is the creator of Jimmy Dean Foods and a country singer.

The value of old age depends upon the person who reaches it. To some men of early performance it is useless. To others, who are late to develop, it just enables them to finish the job.

—THOMAS HARDY

I never thought that at the close of my life, I would be living in a retirement home. But I am. We are bonded together here, needs and age being the glue.

They say that when you get old, learning becomes more difficult. Living the way I live, however, each day is a constant learning experience. I have learned to live with strangers, to make friends, to write stories about my life, to relax and enjoy these rich bonus years. I no longer have to cook my meals nor do my laundry—all of that is done for me, and that's a good thing. It is hardly necessary to read the paper (but I do) because each week I attend a current events class. When I learn about people in other countries and the hardships they endure, I remind myself how lucky I am to live in America.

Who says older people can't learn? Among many other things, I've learned to no longer fear the words old age or retirement homes. Not bad for an eighty-seven-year-old woman.

—**SADE MILLER,** born April 4, 1915, managed properties and ran an office supply business with her husband; she has one son.

∾

Coming of age is something I had always wanted. Since I had been patted on top of my head and told "Never change" for so many years, I thought that coming of age would finally make me feel "intelligent and mature" (whatever that means).

Well, here I am, mature, and I'm not disappointed. This is the best life I've ever had. Coping with everything is so much easier than it used to be. Much of this relatively new freedom and awareness and happiness I owe to my dear husband, Dick, and the rest I will take credit for.

Age, for me, has allowed worries to take a backseat. Any worry—I now call it "concern"—I may have seems as though I've already been there, done that, and survived. Things that used to cause a lot of stress rarely seem so important, and I'm aware that the problems will be solved in due time.

Life just seems to be easier the older I get, as long as I have my health and dear friends to share it, during this wonderful time of my life.

If I had known that "coming of age" would be this good, I would have done it sooner.

—**JANE POWELL,** born April 1, 1928, is a singer and dancer best known for her roles in movie musicals such as *Seven Brides for Seven Brothers.*

∾

*O*ne of the great things about getting older is that you can actually do and think what you want to because you don't have to worry what anyone else thinks of you—because you know who you are.

—**ARLINE TYSZKA,** born May 8, 1926, is a retired registered nurse, mother of three daughters, and grandmother of two granddaughters.

∾

*Y*our memories are yours, relive them as often as you can. Happy memories never wear out.

—**JOYCE BEAUREGARD,** born October 2, 1937, worked in the health care industry in skilled nursing facilities as an administrative assistant both in California and Massachusetts. She recently married her high school sweetheart after finding him more than forty years later.

∾

I've found an interesting paradox now that my body and I have reached this stage of my life. Okay, so my many doctors and I are having to do somewhat more repair work to stave off some of my deterioration, and my hope is that I never need to wear a sign: *"Caution! This Property Is Condemned."* Still, life just keeps getting better and better.

Naturally life isn't so much more fun now because of my slowly growing state of disrepair, but—simply put—the joys enormously outweigh the oys, and the joys are so many. I have the leisure to enjoy my friends and family and to make new friends. I have more time for my very dear children and much more time to spend with my absolutely remarkable (truly!) grandchildren in Florida. There are the time and means to pursue old and new interests. I'm on the Internet now and totally addicted to playing Scrabble with my computer companion. I've enjoyed such volunteer work as recording for people who are blind or dyslexic, and have gone back to writing poetry and to playing the piano. I've taken two drawing classes (where, by the way, our male model wore not so much as a fig leaf—a sight I hadn't seen for quite a while).

Some of the oys, though? Here's a little example: Me—*I'm* the little example! Meet "The Incredible Shrinking Woman." While I was never really tall (okay, I was 4 feet, 11¾ inches), I find my osteoporosis causing me to become more vertically challenged with every passing year. I'm now down to four feet ten inches and soon might just be needing a ladder to board the subway and a parachute or bungee rope for jumping off.

But I enjoy my membership in OWL, a women's advocacy organization, attend the Legislative Caucus on Older Citizens' Concerns at the Massachusetts State House, and am active in a local civic association. Being in a terrific humor-writing group got me started on writing essays, and for the first time in my sixty-eight years I was recently published! I've returned to the study of Yiddish and have written poems and essays in that incomparable language. Also, I'm hoping to join an advocacy group soon as a volunteer in the field of mental health, which I hope may utilize my very fulfilling experience of decades as a psychiatric nurse.

Waiting for another oy? Know the expression

"Different strokes for different folks"? Well, I've been there and done that—though fortunately my strokes have been of the mini variety called TIAs (transient ischemic attacks), which started after my left carotid artery totally occluded and went out of business. Thanks to meds, no longer a problem!

And insomnia? No problem there. I can always be lulled to sleep by the gentle clicking of my prosthetic heart valve.

Still—I now have time in the morning, if I choose, to cook up a scrumptious pot of spaghetti and sauce for breakfast, and the enviable luxury of looking out my windows on a wintry morning to admire the beauty of glistening snow and ice without having to go out into it, risking my neck or tush. In short, life to me is unequivocally joyful.

Okay—so my memory? It should only rest in peace. I believe that that missing part is likely the result of my open-heart surgery, when a few rather useful neurons may have abandoned their hippocampus home in my poor little dome. An example? Let me tell you, it's hard to find your glasses when you're wearing them; they're not anywhere you look! And then there's the time I was talking to my friend Florence, saying, "Honestly, what's happened to so-and-so's mother-in-law is so sad! I know she's over ninety, but her mental faculties have taken such a dive! She asks the same questions over and over, though they've been answered repeatedly. I mean her memory is completely gone, poor woman!" Imagine my embarrassment when I then had to ask (sheepishly!), "Uh—Florence? *What was* my point in *telling* you about this?"

But who cares? I most certainly don't, and that's one of the joys, too. I've always been able to laugh at myself, and oh do I provide myself with *plenty* of material now.

I only hope it's a long time before that wrecking ball comes swinging my way.

—**TALA M. LIPSHUTZ,** born November 8, 1933, is a retired psychiatric nurse.

∽

I have never wanted to be a day older than I am today. It's probably not a usual thing, but I can remember, when I was fifteen, not being anxious to be sixteen, though that of course meant I would be able to drive. I knew that day would come, but I sensed I would never have the current day again, and would one day wistfully wish I could be fifteen again.

I know that's peculiar.

About three years ago I "came out of the closet" at a senior run event, a 10K, I believe, confessing that I am indeed a senior, and have been for several years.

I'm even happily accepting senior discounts at movie theaters and other places.

I still feel young, still treasure each minute of every day, and am not anxious for tomorrow to arrive. I'm trying to savor each minute and each day while I have it—and I do believe my senses have all been heightened to a considerable degree. Colors and scents and God's beauty all around me, as well as the unexpected surprises and delights in people, I seem to experience more deeply than ever. I guess that's one of the "perks" of practice and passing time.

Mostly, though, I'm beginning to get excited (and this seems a little against the trend) about getting closer to home. I know I have a boyhood home in Nashville and a wonderful home in Beverly Hills of some forty-two years now, I'm talking about my heavenly home, and a mansion that I know is waiting for me. Jesus said explicitly, "I go to prepare a place for you; in my Father's house are many mansions." Mama and Daddy are already occupying one of those mansions, and I'm praying that Shirley's and my house will be very close, at least in the same neighborhood as Mama and Daddy's.

Quite seriously, I think getting older and facing the inevitable (I have actually written and recorded a song called "Everybody Dies") would be bleak and frightening indeed—if it weren't for the blessed assurance that what God's Son came to do, He has accomplished, and an indescribable new existence is waiting. I honestly get a little tingly thinking about it.

—**PAT BOONE,** born June 1, 1934, is a songwriter, singer, and actor.

~

*O*ne time my four-year-old granddaughter was staying at my house. In the morning she asked if I was going to work today. I explained to her that I was retired and don't go to work. She asked, "Grammy, what does retire mean?" Then I asked her what she thought retire meant. Sara said, "Well, it's when you get up in the morning and you're tired and you go back to bed." How true.

—**DOLORES E. KWASNY,** born February 21, 1927, is a retired teacher and mother of two children and grandmother of three.

~

*G*etting older is the best revenge.

—**TONY CURTIS,** born June 3, 1925, is an actor.

~

"Snow on the Roof"

With age comes a whitening
That some may find frightening,

Still others enlightening,
I'm told it's been said.
So, enjoy, if you will,
Being "over the hill,"
'Cause you'll find "gray" is still
So much better than just being dead.
No, it won't go away.
So take pride in that gray;
Let it help make your day.
But don't let it go to your head.

—**BOB WOMBACHER, JR.**, born January 4, 1927, is a
World War II veteran and now owns and operates Bashful
Bob's Motel in Arizona as well as a poetry website at
www.lightverse.net.

~

When I was growing up, the thought of someone aged seventy was coupled with images of incapacity and irrelevance. Having reached that age myself this year, I realize how inaccurate those images were. To be sure, we all, sooner or later, reach an age when we begin to slow down. But as the years advance, I find myself more appreciative of everyday joys, especially the companionship of those I love. In an ironic way, my capacity for true enjoyment seems to have deepened with age.

The blessings of family and loved ones have always been particularly enriching. Memories of times

"*My inner child just turned sixty-five.*"

spent with my wife, children, and grandchildren are among my most valued treasures. Simple events and conversations of the past increase in value as I recollect them in later years. How often my beloved wife of thirty-nine years and I reminisce about the exciting and challenging opportunities we have been granted. And how often we thank God for giving us each other to provide the balance and inspiration necessary to persevere when the going gets tough.

Four fine sons, two superb daughters-in-law, and now six grandchildren have been a special blessing to us. They assure that life is never dull. Our vicarious participations in their lives let us share in the fulfillment of every passing grade, each goal scored or starring role, each friendship cemented, and a succession of job opportunities and residential acquisitions and improvements. Our congratulations—and commiserations over inevitable disappointments—have always been graciously received.

Such bonds are a two-way street. For my seventieth birthday, for example, my oldest son collected a list of "Greatest Hits—70+ Memories of My Dad," which he shared with all of us. Even the most dimly remembered of these events sprang to vivid reality with only a little prompting. Some were truly hilarious. And all contributed to a tapestry of remembrance more valuable than any tangible gift could be.

To further the celebration of my seventieth birthday, another son arranged a "surprise trip"—our destination undisclosed until the morning of our departure. It was, he said, to be a return to "my roots," nothing more. It was, in fact, a journey to Nashville, where my father, now long deceased, had been born, where my beloved Pittsburgh Pirates have a farm team (which played on the night of our arrival), and which is the home of country music. Our three days together were capped by a Dolly Parton concert at the historic Ryman Auditorium!

A third son works hard to keep me up to speed on the latest developments in the worlds of baseball, college and professional football, ice hockey, and, in particular, the prospects of our hometown Pittsburgh teams. Many a late-night phone call has been spent in celebration of a minor triumph or in despair over a recent reversal by the objects of our adulation. His seventieth-birthday gift to me was a Roberto Clemente bobble-head doll and adjustments he made to my computer so that I can now receive Pirate games in real time.

One of our sons has a disability; he has mental retardation. In many ways, he has contributed the most to my comprehension of the good that can evolve from nearly every situation. He possesses a kind of quiet dignity that, despite his limitations, serves as an inspiration to all who know him. And his own values are very much in order. Recently, when visiting with us, he and I went to the Washington zoo. We saw all the animals and laughed together at the antics of many of them. At the end of our excursion, I asked him what he had liked best about our experience, expecting a reply that took into account the unique characteristics of one or more of the animals we had seen. Instead, he responded, quite simply: "Being with you."

What a precious gift God has given us in life. We all journey together and are sustained and strengthened by wonderful experiences such as these. In the final analysis, the deepest joys are indeed the simple ones and, as they accumulate over the years, we come to look forward to, rather than fear, the next successive milestone. May it ever be so!

—**DICK THORNBURGH**, born July 16, 1932, served as Attorney General of the United States under Presidents Ronald Reagan and George H. W. Bush, Undersecretary General of the United Nations, and governor of Pennsylvania.

∾

*W*ith a hula hoop in your soul, and an ongoing sense of humor in your being, you can cope with the aches, pains, hair and teeth loss, and a fading memory if you can just enjoy being alive.

Fill your days with friends.

Take the time to smell the roses.

And, smile, even though your dentures may slip.

But most of all, you can get away with being feisty. Folks will just chalk it up as a senior falling apart.

—DARCY LEWIS, born April 14, 1924, is a former actress, drama coach, and journalist, and now writes.

∿

I am seventy-seven years old, and I am fortunate enough to live a life that is utterly fascinating to me. Every night, and several times during the day, I look up and say, "Thank you, God." My thanks are for the way my life has turned out. Believe me, it was not always thus. I twice gave serious thought to suicide during long periods of hopelessness, despair, and failure.

Before I was shipped overseas as an eighteen-year-old private in World War II, I was completely convinced that I was going to be killed in battle. On the night before sailing on the troop ship out of Boston, I went to a Gypsy fortune-teller of the crystal ball variety for a two-dollar reading. I asked her if I was going to be killed. She answered in words to this effect: "Oh, no. You are going to have a long life, deeply troubled at times, but the best part of your life will come in the years at the end of it." In those deeply troubled times, which were indeed a part of my life, the words of that Gypsy fortune-teller, faint though they had become in my mind by then, came back to me, and I hung on and persevered. The wisdom that I have to pass on to younger generations is simple: No matter what happens, and terrible things happen to all of us, you *must* get up and go on again, and again and again. Never give up!

In 1982, my only daughter, Dominique Dunne, a beautiful young actress, was viciously murdered. I loved that child with all my heart. Her death and the ludicrous trial that followed changed my life. Before that, I had been a B-level Hollywood film and television producer, a feather in the breeze, floating on high, but not touching the sky. Then, it was as if God took hold of my life and shook it and shook it, until sense prevailed. I came to realize at the age of fifty that I could write and tell what dishonor and vileness I had witnessed in that courtroom, where the rights of the killer exceeded the rights of the victim he had killed. He received two and a half years. In time, I became a public advocate for victims of crime, both on the printed page in my novels, miniseries, magazine articles, and monthly diaries in *Vanity Fair*, as well as a voice on television talk shows with Larry King, Katie Couric, and folks like that. Now I have my own weekly television series entitled *Power, Privilege, and Justice* as well. I have covered most of the high-profile trials of the last twenty years, and my magazine also sends me to some of the most glamorous events in the world to write about. When

I was forty, I didn't accomplish half as much as I do now. It is so wonderful to be able to say, "I love my life." And I do. Oh, I forgot to mention the best part of it all: I have the most delectable granddaughter, Hannah Dunne, age twelve, who is a constant source of joy in my life.

—**DOMINICK DUNNE**, born October 29, 1925, is a journalist and novelist.

∼

*A*t seventy years of age one great thing is that I still have as much to look forward to as I can look back on, just not as many years to do it all in. But that's okay since I now have the knowledge of how to make it all just as pleasant in even a shorter period of time. I'm stronger now than I was at twenty. Then I could carry forty dollars' worth of groceries in my two arms, now I can use just one hand. I can hold any of my eight great-grandchildren on my lap; as a child I didn't have a great-grandfather's lap to set upon. I have seen more inventions created in my lifetime than in any other lifetime before me.

A = Ain't   G = Gett'n   E = Early'r

Nope, it ain't gett'n early'r, just later. But that was true one second after birth, from there on it's all downhill and nothing a person can do to stop that. A person's lifetime is equal only to how it is spent. Setting goals, working hard to achieve them. Accepting reality for what it is and creating within yourself the ability to continue reaching for the stars, for they are all within your reach.

—**JACK LEROY BRYSON**, born April 26, 1932.

To be seventy years old is like climbing the Alps. You reach a snow-crowned summit, and see behind you the deep valley stretching miles and miles away, and before you other summits higher and whiter, which you may have strength to climb, or may not. Then you sit down and meditate and wonder which it will be.

—HENRY WADSWORTH LONGFELLOW

There are some disadvantages to getting older, but there are two great advantages.

One is that you can profit by your mistakes and learn how to be effective and not just "spin your wheels" as you advocate some cause.

Second is when you reach the point of theoretical retirement, as I have done for the Senate. I now work very full-time for Southern Illinois University, where I teach and head a public policy institute. But in addition, because I'm a workaholic by nature, I'm doing a lot of volunteer things both nationally and internationally. I have the luxury of doing what I want and not necessarily what is politically advantageous.

I also find that I can schedule myself and be at a meeting on a Tuesday night at seven o'clock or whatever the time and date may be. When I was in the Senate you never knew when there was some international or domestic crisis or some crisis in your state that caused total disruption of your schedule. I enjoyed my years in the Senate, but I do like the predictability of the schedule I now have.

—**PAUL SIMON,** born November 29, 1928, served in both the Illinois House of Representatives and Senate; was the state's lieutenant governor; and went on to represent Illinois in both the U.S. House of Representatives and Senate.

∼

I think one of the great things about growing older is the understanding I have that learning never stops, and shouldn't. That's why I entered Western Connecticut State University at the age of sixty-nine to pursue a degree in English. I'll admit that this was a daunting decision to make. How would I fare with the younger crowd? I wondered. Could I keep up with the homework? Would I have the energy to carry a full load of studies? Well, I just completed my freshman year with straight

A's, a first-place prize in an essay contest, and a whole lot of optimism and excitement about the future.

I'm taking one semester at a time and, God willing, I'll be seventy-two or seventy-three when I graduate. Is it going to be worth it? It is already.

—CHARLES W. WITTMAN, born December 4, 1932, is a semiretired advertising copywriter and a full-time student at Western Connecticut State University.

∽

I am a registered nurse, eighty-one years young. It is a blessing in some ways and "scary" in others. I don't feel or act my age. Since I was very young, I have always had a sense of humor, and it has only gotten better with age.

I served in World War II and had the privilege of meeting General George Patton coming out of his trailer when we were in Germany stationed at an evacuation hospital.

I also shook hands with John F. Kennedy during his 1960 presidential campaign when he made a stop at the Youngstown Airport in Vienna, Ohio. I also met Adlai Stevenson at the air base in Vienna. And in 2000 I had the chance to visit with then Attorney General Janet Reno in her office in Washington, D.C. She is a great lady.

All of these were tremendous and thrilling encounters but they pale in comparison with visiting with my four grandchildren. My son Tim and his wife, Marlene, have three girls, Amanda, age five, Cassie, age four, and Alexis, age two. My other son, Bill, and his wife, Kim, have a four-year-old son, Michael. The great thing about getting older and having them around is the way your heart sings when they say, "I love you, Grandma!" "You'll always be in our hearts!" or "Please tell me another story."

The great thing about getting older and wiser is the fact that young people really seem to enjoy talking with me. I have a million stories to tell, and I enjoy telling them. I tell them to treat life as you would a precious piece of sterling silver. See every day as a gift from God. Try to do good for others, don't do anything that would cause harm to you or those around you, and as you go through life, keep your body and soul polished like a fine piece of silver. Stay active, think young, and never let your body and soul tarnish. I don't see my life as becoming the "Golden Years." I see it as the sterling, shining, and bright part of an extraordinary life. You don't get older, you just get better. Remember to feel the breeze in your face and listen to the song in your heart.

—**VIRGINIA L. WILLIAMS**, born May 27, 1921, is a retired registered nurse.

∾

From most retirees I hear, "It's tough getting older." For this writer, I feel blessed with a lot more "things" than others nearing eighty-nine. I have lucked out with a few more "bonus" years and I am saddened by the loss of many friends and relatives not so fortunate. Maintaining a good mind and mobility has been equally rewarding. I've lived to see history in the making, scientific and technological wonders never dreamed of by my ancestors. Childhood memories of horses and wagons, trolley cars, water from a well, and milk from Grandpa's cow are lingering recollections.

When at the tender age of eighty, I learned of computers and how e-mail worked, I was immediately aroused. I had to be in on this. It forever after became the joy of my life. (Not that my lovely wife of sixty-four years rated less.) The availability of communicating instantly with our adult children, our grandchildren, nieces, nephews, a multitude of friends old and new by e-mail is simply priceless.

Now with the acquisition of a digital camera, providing on-screen printable photos with a connection to the computer, and transmission via e-mail to anyone in the world on-line, I find life astonishing.

—**STAN WALLACE,** born December 18, 1913, was self-employed in a small wholesale business that sold candy, tobacco, and sundries to country stores and later became a mutual fund salesman and sales manager.

$\mathcal{F}$irst of all, I've kept working because I love it. Why retire when you love what you're doing? Plus, I don't golf.

But the best part of working once you've reached a "certain age" is the remarkable sense of calm that comes with experience. You recognize situations that may have incited panic in your younger, less mature days.

Once you've seen the movie for the third time, you learn not to sweat the scary parts so much. You become more perceptive to the nuances in certain scenes that you might have missed the first time around. And you react accordingly.

You have a certain historical perspective, which you keep in mind when you see people getting positively excited about things that you know aren't going to work, or negatively excited about things that you know are simply going to run their course.

As you grow older, you learn to take the breathless cover words of news magazines less and less seriously. It's very soothing.

—ROBERT A. LUTZ, born February 12, 1932, is General Motors Vice Chairman, Product Development, and Chairman, GM North America.

*A*t age nineteen I thought I knew it all. At age seventy-six I've discovered that there is much yet to learn and much to enjoy in life. Set a goal or several goals for your future and work toward them. Get a good education in whatever field you are interested in or have an aptitude for. Don't let failure deter you, you can try until you succeed. Give praise when it is deserved. If you criticize, do it in a constructive way, and don't take constructive criticism as a put-down. Life has its ups and downs, so be strong in adversity and humble in success. Choose your words carefully, for once spoken they remain forever. You can stay young as you grow older by living a healthy life: Eat nutritious food, exercise regularly, do not indulge in destructive habits. Prepare for retirement with a variety of activities that you enjoy.

—**CLARENCE BURGEMAN,** born October 17, 1925, is a former business partner with his father and most recently retired as a sales representative for the Illinois state lottery.

∾

"I'm Beautiful"

My little eyes are beautiful
Because I still can see,
My funny legs are beautiful
Because they carry me,

And because it's mostly there,
I can love my once-red hair.

My hands may sometimes fail me,
But still I have and hold,
My whimsical feet
Are a wonder to behold,
And I'm happy to relate
That my aching back is straight.

As for my falling face,
I'm not afraid to show it;
Accustomed to my face
Are so many glad to know it.

And the beauty of my brain,
Being human, has been shown
(though I sometimes think my brain
has a mind of its own).

I may not have exactly
The shape of my youth,
But I try to stay in shape
And accept nature's truth.

To gravity and time,
My body must be dutiful,

But I can't complain—
Though it does sound vain,
I'm beautiful.

—**ANNIE W. SMALL,** born June 24, 1923, is a retired
executive secretary and a late-blooming poet and photo-
graphic artist who runs the website www.smallstudio46.com/
ASHome.htm.

~

*Y*ou grow up! You stop putting the blame of "if,
when, or why," on others and put the responsibility of circumstances that have happened
throughout life on yourself. With this catharsis
you find freedom! You learn to like yourself and you
suddenly feel young again. You can say what you
think without the fear of losing a friend, for if it's a
true friend, he will accept you for the way you are.
The same applies to your siblings. There is no way
you can change others' way of thinking—accept
them as they are, as they must do the same for you,
otherwise, distance yourself from them. Life is too
short to waste time trying to please everyone, for
you have places to go and things to do—what other
generation of senior citizens had as much freedom
to do and places to go, to do whatever it is they
would like to do, with whoever they want to do it
with! We get ten to fifteen percent discounts at the

department and grocery stores, free dinner, shows, and money back at the casinos (but then I always say the senior bus trips are what keep the casinos open), we have wonderful senior centers where you can take classes in writing, woodcarving, crafts, or yoga, play pool, play bingo, have a well-balanced lunch for $1.25 (you pay only what you can afford) and have free coffee and donuts every morning compliments of the local stores, and day-old bread, rolls, and cakes, and other things too numerous to mention. There is no reason for anyone to go hungry or be alone in today's world. If you keep an open mind, have a sense of humor, reach out to others for friendship, and most important of all, pray for others and keep God in your heart, then you'll find the greatest things about getting older are having friends and family to share it with—and doing what you damn well please—no explanation necessary!

The greatest realization came as I got older (matured), when I knew I could take all the things that I had put on the "back burner" waiting for that one day I would have the time to do what I liked. With age came the confidence in myself to apply for a job I had no experience in, to believe in the confidence a friend had in me to become an astrologer, and while recovering from surgery, having the confidence to write and submit an article that would be published. My three minutes of fame came when I was pulled up on stage to sing with one of the owners of a dinner theater, and the confidence to carry through, another dream come true. The worst that could happen is to make a fool of myself, and if it would make someone laugh, that would be good, for laughter is the best medicine. All this I would never have had the courage to even think of doing when I was younger, so I have found the greatest thing about getting old is learning to have confidence to do whatever I desire and learn to truly accept and like myself. For if I don't like me, how can I expect others to? Life is too precious to dwell on the negative, and much too short, therefore I try to live each day to its fullest. Being a widow, having friends to share things with is the greatest! I have Parkinson's, and although it has slowed me down somewhat, it hasn't got me down. I still drive my own car, shop, clean, cook, travel, write, and go to Atlantic City to the casino to see the shows and gamble a bit—you might say I go to make a deposit!

—ELLAMAY (MOFFETT) CIAUDELLI, born November 25, 1931, was a full-time homemaker who raised two children.

❧

*W*illard asked me what words of wisdom I have to pass on to the younger generation. I have found that the secret of staying young is to live honestly, eat slowly, and lie about your age. Seriously though, and I say this with all sincerity, if you always remain cool and never lose your enthusiasm—then the world is yours. And it doesn't matter what people say about you. Your friends won't believe it and your enemies already know it.

I remember being asked on my seventy-fifth birthday at the Friars Club if there were to be candles on the cake. I said, "No, it's a birthday party, not a torchlight procession!"

Someone asked me what was so great about turning seventy-five. I said, "No more calls from insurance agents."

I thank my mother for my great genes. When she turned ninety years of age, she went to the doctor for an examination and he said, "You're doing wonderful, you're in great shape. I want you walking five miles a day." She said, "Okay." She's ninety-five today and we don't know where the hell she is!

—**SOUPY SALES,** born January 8, 1926, is a comedian and radio personality.

∾

The great things for me in getting older and at the ripe old age of eighty-one consist of so many wonderful things that have happened to me here in my golden years, especially the kindness, trust, and most of all—the tremendous amount of genuine love from my two children and their children, my grandchildren. My excellent health has been a Godsend to me, and I thoroughly enjoy life to its fullest. There are times when I feel guilty to see so many younger people suffering with incurable diseases and their lives shattered with no light at the end of the tunnel, and them knowing their lives will be shortened. I think many times it should be me instead of those who are so much younger than I. I'm assuming that God has plans for all and He'll do what is right; we must trust to His good judgment and continue on with our journey.

Getting older is rewarding to us seniors for having the wisdom that we can very often share with so many younger people. It's very gratifying to us and we feel we've accomplished another milestone in our long lives.

—**RUTHE WILLIAMS,** born July 8, 1921, owned and operated a home beauty salon while raising two children as a single mom; before retiring she joined a large international hair cosmetic company and traveled extensively working as a district supervisor in sales and teaching licensed hairdressers to become hair colorist technicians.

~

*N*othing in the world can take the place of persistence.

Talent will not—nothing is more common than unsuccessful men with talent.

Genius will not—unrewarded genius is almost a proverb.

Education alone will not—the world is filled with educated derelicts. Persistence and determination alone are omnipotent!

I read that message on my show every day for a week and received a tremendous response. I told Ray Kroc that it must have struck a familiar chord with everyone.

He then printed it up and posted it on the wall of every McDonald's around the world.

It certainly was a big part of my philosophy when I got diabetes at age eight. My doctor told my mother I would be lucky if I reached nine. But even at that tender age I wanted to prove them wrong, and I have—thanks to God, persistence, determination, and the love of family, daily exercise, and vitamin B. I'm now in my early sixties. I still play basketball full court for two hours twice a week, watch my diet, take my insulin, and continue my work in the entertainment business.

I've been fortunate to log in over 15,000 radio

shows (local and national), over 25,000 commercials, been a regular on fourteen national TV series (including *Rowan & Martin's Laugh-in*—every show), over 1,000 national TV shows (including a TV special with Willard Scott), and over 3,000 animated cartoon episodes starting in 1962 (including *The New Alan & Brady Show* for Carl Reiner).

I take time every day to grab some endorphins listening to music (Don Costa's *Umbrellas of Cherbourg* album is one of my favorites), walking along a tree-lined street, spending time next to the ocean, hearing the scrunch of leaves underfoot in the autumn, and perusing antiquarian bookstores, satisfying my curiosity to learn more each twenty-four hours.

I try to make the most of each moment. Joy is so powerful, we're only given a little bit each day— try to find it!

—**GARY OWENS,** born May 10, 1936, has been an announcer, host, or entertainer in thousands of radio and television programs and movies.

∼

*N*umber one on the list has to be it is more interesting than I thought it would be, and in my case, a lot more peaceful. I am a seventy-one-year-old female and the mother of four. I worked from age fourteen to age sixty-five, with some time off for having children. I enjoyed my busy years and I consider that a big factor in the enjoyment of these years. I can remember at age sixty-five or sixty-six that for the first time I was a bit out of step with the world—the speed of the drivers, rudeness in overcrowded grocery stores, and at that time life handed me a wheelchair (arthritis) and solved my problem. I live alone and like it, but have family nearby. I have the time to enjoy things that busier people my age don't have time for. Sunrises are beautiful. Thinking is fun. Learning to cook for one and having it be both nourishing and inexpensive was a great challenge.

The biggest surprise of growing old was that so many things have stayed the same in my brain. A good-looking young man is still good to look at, a thunderstorm is still scary even though I have learned all about them, and a good piece of cherry pie never diminishes in taste. I love Monday morning with no alarm clock. I would have to say the nicest part of growing old in my case is the lack of time constrictions. I really can read my book *all day* if I wish to do so. Tonight I can cook a full meal for myself *or* if the lazies set in or I stay on the phone too long, then I can have a bowl of good cereal and a piece of fruit. Old age offers more flexibility.

My life is not perfect; I did not plan too wisely in the cost of growing old. But being born during the Depression and raised by a mom who got great mileage out of her groceries, I find myself doing the same. The secret, of course, is to do the work yourself. Fast food or defrost and eat is not part of my life.

To summarize, it is in my opinion, growing old happily is just the next step in enjoying life in the younger years. Take the time to be pleasant and loving while you are on the trip to growing old. I cannot promise that it will be returned to you, but you will feel good in your middle.

—MARY E. CANTACESSI, born March 2, 1931, was an office manager for a small certified public accounting firm and also raised four children.

When I was young I was amazed at Plutarch's statement that the elder Cato began at the age of eighty to learn Greek. I am amazed no longer. Old age is ready to undertake tasks that youth shirked because they would take too long.

—W. SOMERSET MAUGHAM

When asked quickly to tell great things about aging, I would have to wonder what they could possibly be.

At ninety-five there are times that there are none at all. Luckily you don't stop there. You think of senior discounts for free coffee, but you really don't crave coffee much anymore. You can also get into the movies about two dollars cheaper, but you don't go so much because you don't hear so well.

Sort of shallow incentives, but incentives nevertheless.

You are no longer involved in guiding your children, grandchildren, and even great-grandchildren, as they are telling you what to do now. "Come on, Grandma," as my two-year-old great says as she wishes to get me to move.

You receive all kinds of humorous poems about aging at which you can laugh. However, there is too much truth that hits home to laugh heartily.

You can sit for a long time and not feel like you are useless. You are recuperating for the next foray. It may be just getting up.

As to advice for the younger ones, all I can say is live each day to the fullest and hope that you will age gracefully.

There is nothing you can do about getting older, so take it as it comes.

Do the best that you can with a great big smile.

—**EVALINE GILL,** born February 18, 1907, worked as a teacher for thirty years before she retired; she also raised two children alone and now has three grandchildren and five great-grandchildren.

The time is now.
The past is prologue, they say.
The future has not yet committed.
The present is touchable.
Engage it.

—**DICK LOCHER,** born June 4, 1929, is best known as the illustrator of the cartoon "Dick Tracy" and is a winner of the Pulitzer Prize.

～

We thought a long time about how to explain the philosophy of life as it pertains to Aubrey and Ann Roberts and what has made us what we are today. And I suppose this is the best explanation we can come up with.

Face life straight on. Good or bad, you are going to have to face it, and if you see it coming in the door and it doesn't slip up from behind, you have a better chance of dealing with it. And deal with it, you will. You may not like it, but it is there. Whether it be good times or bad times, it is there for you to face.

As senior citizens, we have seen about all there is to see of life. We were never the kind of people to sit in a corner and crochet, if you will. Aubrey is a musician and bandleader and also held a regular job

to support a wife and four children. I worked for a railroad for many years until retirement. And we are both still able to do the things we enjoy. He is still playing his music and I am involved with my art, only I do it digitally now instead of with watercolor and oils.

Aubrey was the oldest of six children. When he was eight years old, his father was killed in an accident, leaving his mother with no income or help of any kind. He assumed the role of helper and through this he came to the music. He found when he was fourteen he could make fifteen dollars a night playing fiddle at country dances. The most he could make plowing for someone was a dollar a day. So he came to music, which is his one love.

I was an only child, without even a first cousin. When I finished high school at sixteen, I got a job. Back then, a girl either got married or got a job. There was no money for further education, but I managed to get a fair education through correspondence schools and night schools.

We have seen our loved ones die and leave us. We are the oldest survivors of either of our families. We lost our parents, siblings, some children and grandchildren and friends. How it hurt to lose people we loved. We felt the loss, but still we wouldn't sit with our backs to the door.

In 1969, I was involved in an automobile accident.

A drunk driver hit us from behind. My father was killed, and I suffered a broken back and still wear a brace, but we faced it and went on from there. It is painful, but I have not allowed it to take priority in my life, and have learned to cope with it without the use of drugs.

The worst time was when Aubrey had to have brain surgery in 1996 and the struggle back to a normal life. We faced it and were up to the challenge. There is very little he is limited in his ability to do. He cannot lift over twenty pounds, but who wants to pick up sacks of cement anyway! We started putting even more effort into the music and are now the best-known Western Swing dance band in the vicinity.

We also do a lot of charity work for the disabled and elderly. And through this connection, Aubrey was nominated for the "hero of the year" award in 2001. We proudly display the certificate in our studio.

In our many years on earth, there have been many challenges and triumphs, and never once did we shirk or shun them. And we feel it was simply because we weren't sitting with our backs to the door.

—**ANN ROBERTS,** born July 25, 1931, worked for a major railroad as a telegraph operator/agent as well as a radio/helicopter/ambulance dispatcher for a hospital; and
AUBREY ROBERTS, born August 11, 1927, worked as a supervisor in a furniture factory as a color expert, did a little farming and raised some cattle, and is a musician.

~

When I began [*Time Flies*] my attitude toward aging was a blend of fighting and accepting it; but in the time it has taken me to write the book, I have gotten older and I'm doing a little more fighting than accepting right now.

"*Dee*-fense!" I am crying to joints that need 3-in-One Oil, to intestines that are begging for custard, and to eyes that are proud of their ability to distinguish day from night. However, I am also counting my blessings and not my time with a pointless pining for yesterday because I keep telling myself, "The older I get, the luckier I am."

Am I aging gracefully? Aging gracefully is for Baryshnikov; Cosby stumbles along, doing as well as he can and doing it in the here and now. The past is a ghost, the future a dream, and all we ever *have* is now. This philosophical flash may belong in a fortune cookie, but it's the best I can do at fifty. I do not know if the days are dwindling to a precious few for me or if I will make it to ninety-eight like my grandfather. Nonetheless, at fifty I am convinced that we must live as if we're immortal. The eminent scientist Linus Pauling says that in a way we *are* immortal because the body keeps renewing itself. And I am cheerfully with you, Linus—my legs are surely ripe for renewing—but you will pardon me if, once in a while, I behave like the *other* Linus and reach for my security blanket.

—**BILL COSBY,** born July 12, 1937, is a comedian whose television program *The Cosby Show* won numerous Emmy Awards during its eight-year run.

～

I am always surprised when someone or something makes me realize that I am now over seventy years old. I feel so much like the young boy I once was. In fact, I still am that boy today.

How can I say this, however, when there are so many things I used to love doing which are now entirely out of my reach. Running in the wet sand, for instance, diving headfirst into the waves and feeling the turmoil of the brine all over my body, or climbing a forest trail in great strides from spruce to spruce. How ever can I claim to be, or feel, the same as I was?

All things considered, it seems to be a mystery.

This doesn't come as a total surprise, though. With the years I have discovered that our lives are full of mystery.

There are those we encounter at each of our first steps. Why does the pretty flame from the match bite my finger when I touch it? Why does the moon become so thin after having been so fat? Why is my room populated with so many monsters that frighten me so much just after Mother switches the light off? Why does the car spring to life once Father gets behind the wheel?

Years go by and these little mysteries disappear along with them. Others appear and I marvel at them. I would like to share a few of them with you.

Of course, there is the mystery of the infinity of space, at once empty and filled with billions and billions of stars. And there is also the infinitely small, even more mysterious, which we are made of.

More so, the mystery of life, this life, where we meet pain and ugliness, happiness and beauty, always together, completing each other even as they oppose each other.

And all the questions we can ask ourselves about these topics receive responses that in turn lead to new questions.

However it is only now, with all those years behind me, that I become more and more conscious that there is something far more inexplicable than all this, and also far more important. To me, it is the greatest of all mysteries.

I am talking about the mystery of love.

Whether love inspires us or not can make every moment of our lives loaded with unforeseen worth. What appeared like a catastrophe can, with love, become a source of happy times, and our fear for the future can turn into confidence in ourselves and in those who surround us.

I would like to share a little story about this.

It starts like many of those fairy tales where good witches turn ugly toads into beautiful young princes, much to the princesses' satisfaction.

Once upon a time, there was a little girl, barely seven years old, who told her parents that when she grew up, she would become a doctor. Her parents smiled and thought nothing more of it. But the little girl continued thinking about it all through the years that took her from elementary school to high school, from childhood to adulthood, when all major decisions are taken.

Having become a beautiful young woman, she started arduous medical studies. One day she finally reached her goal, the one that the little seven-year-old girl had decided to set for herself.

Now she was practicing the profession she had chosen, independent and full of the joy of life. Her father rejoiced in her present happiness and in the prospect of her happiness to come. He could already see her at the side of the man she would love and with whom she would blossom.

The beautiful young woman did indeed fall in love. But the one who would become everything to her was a poor cripple. All that was left of him was what poliomyelitis had left alive from when he had had it as a young child—a poor misshapen body, whose every movement was painful to see, so hard it appeared to make. He could read and write but had not studied further. His family had not known how or been able to give him the means to lead an activity unimpaired by his physical handicap that would enable him to somehow support himself. His mother was dead. His father, already aged, would soon no longer be there to help him.

How could anyone think that he could ever take his place as a husband by the side of this beautiful young woman, make her happy, and bring her the moral and material support that the circumstances of life make necessary between spouses, at one time or another?

The wedding did take place, though. The beautiful young woman, radiating with joy in her immaculate wedding dress, was led by her father to the altar where this poor thing was waiting, wavering in his tuxedo. The father gave his daughter's hand to him, and in doing so lived the sorriest moment of his life. He despaired when he thought of the future that awaited his dearly beloved daughter. How could he think that this union would produce daily bliss, the sharing of deep joys, the comfort of being side by side to face the difficult or tragic moments that life holds in store. He was convinced that this wedding could only lead to failure, which he suffered in advance to see his daughter go through.

The newlyweds left for another city, where the bride had a position in a hospital. The father thought of his daughter and feared for her the future that he could foretell.

But he was wrong. Love is powerful when it is true.

As it happens in all fairy tales, this true love changed the "cripple" into a husband, and soon, a father, who was perfectly capable of making his wife very happy. They organized their daily activities in the joy of being together, and the husband, despite his physical limitations, took his rightful place in them.

And the father, now a grandfather, while playing with his grandchildren, meditated on the mystery of love.

You don't believe in fairy tales and mysteries? You can safely believe in this one. Because I am that father, and that woman is my daughter.

—**GERARD DAMERVAL,** born June 24, 1931, is a retired agronomist engineer who has four children, eight grandchildren, and a wife of forty-five years.

∽

*T*here are two words that grow more important as one gets older. They are—"over" and "next."

That great Saturday night is *over* as soon as you get into the car to drive home. Best to recognize that and lean into *next*.

That is what living in the moment is all about.

—**NORMAN LEAR,** born August 27, 1922, is a television producer of dozens of programs, among them *All in the Family*.

∽

*O*ne of the advantages of getting older is that you have more time to enjoy nature. When I was working and raising a family, I was too busy to stop and look around and enjoy my surroundings. Now I can pause, relax and look up at the sky, and appreciate the beauty around me. Another plus to being a senior is that I have the luxury of choosing to do—or not do—whatever I want, whenever I want.

—**CHARLOTTE NEDELL,** born October 7, 1902, worked for Kings County Trust Company, now HSBC Bank, until her retirement at age sixty-five; however, the bank asked her to return to work, and she stayed there until her second retirement at age eighty.

∽

*W*hen I woke up this morning I was eighty. Talk about the speed of light. How about the speed of age! It seems only a few years ago that I was catching fireflies, flying kites, spinning tops, shooting marbles—knucks down, of course—having rubber-gun fights, playing sandlot baseball and football—no adult supervision, if you please—taking in the Saturday cinema serial—*The Galloping Ghost* starring Red Grange was my favorite—and hunting and fishing on nearby rivers and streams.

My dad taught me to handle a rifle and a shotgun when I was ten. During hunting season, one of my chores after school was to bag some game for the table. No, I'm not making this up. You may remember that in the early 1930s the economy was in the tank, and my family was feeling the pinch. When I recall that time, I comment that things were so tough around our house that when my dad threw the dog a snack, it had to signal for a fair catch!

Other than our homegrown chickens, my dad's expertise with a gun and a fishing rod provided just about all the meat served on our table. I did bring home a few "keepers," however, and had my first lesson in making a contribution to any group effort.

Having reached eighty, I'm well into the fourth quarter of my life. So it's not too early to take inventory. Have I found some benefits that go with aging? What have I done with the time that has been given to me? What have I learned that might benefit others? Let's take a look.

Aging

What are some of the benefits that go with aging? There aren't many. Most will agree that they would just as soon get stuck somewhere between twenty and thirty. But if you are fortunate with your health, there are a few benefits that come to mind.

For one thing, after retirement, you have more time to enjoy your family, your friends, and your personal interests. More time to travel and enjoy what the world has to offer. Perhaps most important, you have more time to spend with your wife to make up for all the time your profession kept you away from home. Additionally, the older you get, the easier it is to shoot your age in golf. And finally, perhaps along the way, you've done and learned some things that might benefit others. Maybe, maybe not. In any event, here are some thoughts.

Goals & Objectives

To accomplish goals and objectives, whether professional or personal, requires commitment, preparation, determination, patience, fortitude, continuous follow-up, and above all, self-discipline. The future belongs to those that "show up on time and make it happen."

Value System

As I write this in 2002, I realize how old-fashioned I must be. I remember when we used to do multimillion-dollar projects on a handshake. We actually thought our employees were our most important asset, and that they, together with our shareholders and the public, should be the beneficiaries of any success we achieved. And I sure don't recall anything called a "golden parachute."

Old-fashioned or not, I still believe that honesty, integrity, and professional ethics are worthwhile guidelines to chart your course. Individuals with no values usually feast on a culture of deceit and greed. They seldom produce anything of long-term value and they usually leave a trail of heartbreak and tears.

Education

A thorough, comprehensive education is so vital to give each of us a jump start in life. When I hear about the current trend in "dumbing down" test standards and "social promotions," I view it as a betrayal of the student. Luckily, I benefited from a different approach.

The public schools I attended all had good curricula—especially in history, science, and math—and a no-nonsense approach to attendance, conduct, and performance testing. With a solid public school education, I was then fortunate to be accepted into an engineering school that had a tough "no quarter given" approach to academic performance. Of the hundred plus engineers in my freshman class, only nineteen of us finished the course. Was it worth all the midnight oil? You bet!

National Service

I was nineteen on December 7, 1941. But because I was in my junior year of engineering, the draft board allowed me to finish in a speed-up program. After completing my courses, I joined the navy and spent thirty-one months in the service with seventeen months of combat duty in the Pacific.

It's not the sort of thing that anyone normally volunteers for. And the survival learning curve has a steep slope. You'd better learn quickly the critical importance of teamwork. Further, the commitment and self-discipline to never let your unit down. Lives, including your own, may depend on how well you do your assigned job. Race, religion, or politics never enter the equation. It's only your performance that counts.

I was fortunate to get out of the war intact. I learned a lot, in particular how to get things done with a melting pot of talents and personalities. It served me well later when as an engineer I was involved in building process plants all over the world.

Community Service

Shortly after I retired, I was given the opportunity to get involved with both the city and the county in a wide range of assignments from planning and zoning to economic development, city council member, airport zoning, property tax appeals, and the like. I've found the work to be most rewarding and an excellent way to give something back to the community. Get involved. You won't regret it. And you can make a difference.

Life Challenges

To me life is sort of like golf. In golf you're going to end up in the rough on many occasions. The important thing is how you play the next shot. Like golf, in life you're going to face many hurdles—some personal, some professional, some physical, some financial. Again, the important thing is how you play the next shot. Hardship and adversity are the true tests of your faith and mettle.

Family

Close, enduring family relations are perhaps life's greatest joy. Happily, in our family, we're all still speaking to one another and we thoroughly enjoy frequent get-togethers.

Health

Life's blessings and achievements can best be enjoyed with good health. Good health is largely hereditary. But individual effort—diet, exercise, and workout programs—accomplish wonders. Commitment and self-discipline are the main requirements.

Faith

I don't begin to fully understand what makes the universe work and our place in the scheme of things. I do believe that there is a force behind it all. And I do know that it is good to have it on your side.

Lessons Learned

Even at eighty you realize that life is short. There is no answer to life. You just live it and make the most of it. A lot depends on you. A little preparation on your part can make a world of difference. And may the Force be with you.

—**RALPH YOUNG,** born November 27, 1922, is a retired registered professional engineer.

~

$\mathcal{S}$ome of my greatest memories are when I was attending my Masonic lodge and enjoying the friendship and fellowship of my fraternal brethren. I still keep in touch with some of them and going over old times sure makes me feel good.

For younger people my words to them is get into some type of activity where you can meet and have friendship together.

Willard, I know you are familiar with what I speak of, and I'm sure it jogs your mind about your days and meetings you attended.

There is no TV show, movie, or other form of

entertainment that can replace a friendly greeting or a welcome handshake you can receive when you become involved in an organization that promotes fellowship.

—**JACK C. STEINMETZ,** born August 10, 1929, is a retired federal employee.

With mirth and laughter let old wrinkles come.
—*MERCHANT OF VENICE*, WILLIAM SHAKESPEARE

I find that when people ask me how old I am, I need to know whether they want my chronological, psychological, or physiological age. As I write this, I am within one month of my seventieth birthday but behave in a manner that still embarrasses our five children and eight grandchildren and am training to run in my sixth marathon for my birthday present.

So I am still learning from senior citizens myself. Lesson number one is that if you do what makes you lose track of time, you are never really working and can't age. After all, if you don't know what time it is, how can you get older? You'll be too busy to age and if you are living your chocolate ice cream, it will never be defined as work. I know from my life and my patients' lives the benefits of living your chocolate ice cream.

Another lesson is to accept your mortality and spend your time doing what feels right and not what you think you should do. Pay attention to the wisdom of your heart and you will also live a longer, healthier life. Learn to say no when you don't want to do something. It gets easier the older you get and the more you appreciate we are all here for a limited time. As my ninety-three-year-old mother advises, "When you have a decision to make, do what makes you happy."

Remember that pain is necessary but suffering is optional. Use your pain to direct, define, and protect you. You do that by having what I call happy depressions. Charcoal under pressure can become a diamond. So learn from your pain and let it teach and direct you. Then you don't get depressed about being depressed but ask what changes you need to make in your life when you don't feel good. Or as my mom says, "God is redirecting you. Something good will come of this."

Eliminate the things in your life that affect your health adversely. The other problems are solved by bringing love into the situation. Kill with kindness, torment with tenderness, and as you age develop love blindness. It doesn't see faults and is less of a problem than glaucoma or macular degeneration. I find amnesia works well, too, when loving is difficult, and the older you get, the easier it is to forget. Being married to the same woman for forty-eight years, I appreciate how amnesia has benefited our relationship, as has our love.

You change your life by rehearsing and practicing being the person you want to be. If you are depressed act as if you were Lucille Ball in one of her *I Love Lucy* shows. If you don't like that, ask yourself, as I do in difficult situations, "What would Lassie do?" Pick a role model, if Lassie doesn't suit you, and rehearse and practice.

Learn to transcend your problems as my ninety-five-year-old mother-in-law did. When I asked her what she wanted me to pray for her, as she sat in a wheelchair in a nursing home, she answered, "World peace."

Learn to be free of fear. There is nothing that you will encounter that you cannot handle. Others have shown you that with their lives. When I asked a ninety-three-year-old patient of mine suffering from gallstones and cancer what she was afraid of, she paused for a few moments and then answered, "Driving on the parkway at night."

Look where you are going. When a researcher at Yale asked a ninety-seven-year-old man how he kept from falling, he said, "I look where I am going."

Learn to be yourself. When I ask residents in

nursing homes to draw pictures of themselves at age forty-five and now, I usually get two pictures—the age forty-five one shows a thin smiling person, and the present age is a fat and unhappy one. Bill gave me one picture of a happy smiling face and when I said I asked for two drawings, he said, "That's me then and that's me now."

Learn to see beauty. A blind widow was admitted to a nursing home a week after her husband died and said, "What a beautiful place." They said, "You can't see and you just came in the door. How do you know what the place is like?" She said, "I have a choice as to what I see." As Helen Keller said, "Keep your face to the sunshine and you cannot see the shadows."

Do not hide your wounds. When people ask me, "How are you?" I say, "Depressed. Out of my anti-depressant and my doctor's away so I can't renew my prescription." Eighty percent respond, "I know how you feel." Then therapy begins.

So remember in love's service only the wounded soldier can serve. If you don't like my style, then walk with a cane and wear a bandage, and everyone will share their wounds with you.

My father-in-law, at age seventy, fell and injured his spine when he started wearing bifocals. He became a quadriplegic and was an inspiration to us all, dying at age ninety-seven. I asked him for advice for the elderly and he said, "Tell them to fall on something soft." A few days later he said, "It doesn't always work. They stood me up in therapy and I fell over on my wife and broke her leg. So tell them to just fall up." I thought that was a joke until the night he told us he was tired of his body and was skipping his vitamins and dinner. He died quietly that evening. By my definition he just fell up and once again became dreamless, unalive, and perfect. You are capable of doing that, too, when you tire of your body, as long as family is willing to let go.

On my father-in-law's headstone it reads: "He Just Fell Up." My mother-in-law, whenever her birthday arrived, would always say, "My age is not a matter for discussion." No matter how proud we were of all her years, that was her statement at every birthday party. When she died, at age ninety-five, I wanted to leave off the year of her birth and engrave that sentence on her headstone, but the family voted for "The Nightingale Rests," which was related to her operatic singing career. I think we all need to come up with a one-liner for our headstones. Like, "Now maybe they'll believe I was really sick" or "I had 35 wonderful years of married life and 35 out of 48 isn't too bad," or something inspirational if it fits your lifestyle.

The last bit of advice I would offer you is about how to die laughing. First embarrass your children regularly so that you will give them the gift of your being blamed for their behavior. What our children hear when they do something strange is, "Do you know who his father is?" That lets them off the hook.

Now presuming you have accomplished what you came to earth to accomplish, when you get tired of your body, gather your loved ones and tell them to tell stories about your life. If you follow my instructions, you will hear things that will allow you to die laughing. So serve the world in your way and when you get tired, go out with a smile.

—**DR. BERNIE SIEGEL,** born October 14, 1932, is a physician, patient advocate, founder of EcaP, Exceptional Cancer Patients, and author of several best-selling books, including *Love, Medicine & Miracles: Lessons Learned About Self-Healing from a Surgeon's Experience with Exceptional Patients* and *Peace, Love & Healing: Bodymind Communication and the Path to Self-Healing: An Exploration.*

∼

J had no idea what joy I would be blessed with when our first and subsequent grandchildren were born. As we watch them grow, my wife and I have learned to listen to the wisdom and magic that comes out of their little mouths. Our hearing might be failing, but it doesn't matter because I can hear the caring and love in the voice of one little honest girl who tells me all in one breath that I have a big

fat belly and that she will always love me to the moon and back. Yes, we have learned to listen to those little ones repeat our words as they tell us to buckle up, look both ways before we cross the street, and other small reminders that we have played a part in their precious lives. We bless the years and tears it has taken to get where we are today—our tired old ears now let us hear enough to realize that we are rich in flesh and blood courtesy of our precious granddaughters and grandson. Our hearing isn't failing; it just makes us listen a little harder to the truly important things in life.

—JOHN (JEFF) FENNELL, born March 21, 1937.

∾

Our middle school–aged granddaughter's class was studying aging. That's a politically correct term for getting old. One of the assignments for the class was to interview a grandparent or other older person to get some perspective on the subject.

Our granddaughter came to us with a list of twenty questions. They started out with such things as: "Where were you born?" "When were you born?" "How old were you when you had your first date?" Then came question number twenty—"Is aging fun?"

"Is aging fun?" I repeated with a hysterical laugh.

Now, like I said, "aging" is a politically correct term for getting old. What she was really asking was, "Is it fun being old?" From my response to her question, I'm sure she figured I thought it was.

First of all, I suppose whether or not you think it is fun depends on what your life has been like and whether you get to the "being old" stage in fairly good health. Also, who decides when you are old? I may have reached the stage of having a Medicare identification card, but I don't feel old. I'm still a very active person. I am enjoying pretty good health. I still have my spouse of almost fifty years to share my life, plus I have a bevy of wonderful, supportive family and friends.

I have learned from reaching this exalted age, however, that it is not fun having arthritis, cataracts, high blood pressure, false teeth, hearing aids, ad infinitum. Also, if I had not been having a "senior moment" (I got that phrase from Cousin Lura in Ohio) or a "lapse synapse" (I got that phrase from a book by Effie Leland Wilder, and if you don't know what a synapse is, look it up)—anyway, like I was saying, if I could have thought quickly enough, I would have asked my granddaughter if I could address her class and give them some insight into aging.

All of us are aging from the day we are born.

When we are young, we look at older people, especially those who have frequent "senior moments" when their brain just won't bring up needed information, and we snicker behind our hands, or give knowing looks at our friends that say: "That old person is weird. She's losing it." But when we are that older person, we know that some things happen not because we are weird, but because Father Time has caught up with us and we can't function like we did when we were young.

For example, young people think it is funny to cup a hand behind an ear and say, "Eh?" But not being able to hear is very frustrating, both for the hearing-impaired person and for those who must constantly repeat information or listen to strange answers that come because the person did not hear the question properly. And don't say, "Why doesn't she get a hearing aid?" I know persons who have tried several, including some very expensive ones that did not solve the problem. Also, I know from my older perspective that when a wife answers every question asked of her husband, it isn't because she is trying to take charge of her husband's life. It's because she knows he didn't hear the question.

Another thing I have learned is not to be too critical when I see an older woman with too much blush on her cheeks, eyebrows that need shaping, unkempt fingernails, etc., because I have learned from experience what poor eyesight, arthritis, and other things can do to affect one's ability to do personal grooming. Not everyone can afford to have someone do it for them, either.

And then there is the problem of not being able to move very fast. We get in the way sometimes of young people who want to go faster. Well, let me tell you, boys and girls, your life will pass quicker than you can imagine. Slow down a little bit. Take some time to talk to some of us "aging folk." We have "been there, done that, and got the T-shirt" (I forget where I heard that quote). We lived before television, computers, space travel, jet planes, and a lot of other stuff you take for granted. You might find it interesting to know how we handled life when we were your age, and you might learn some things that would help you as you "age."

Is aging fun? I guess it mostly depends on whether you still have your sense of humor. I hope I never lose my ability to laugh at things. I will let you know when I get old just how it feels. Just be charitable toward all of us old ones. You will be there before you know it. Time flies when you're having fun.

Like I said, if I could have thought quickly enough, I would have told all these things to my granddaughter's class. Now that I have placed my thoughts on paper, do I think they will read them? Who am I kidding!

—**GLORIA L. MUNN,** born December 14, 1933, is a retired health insurance claims processor.

∾

*B*est thing about being old? Freedom and time to do what you enjoy most—maybe even being lazy! How about breakfast at 2:00 P.M.? Wisdom for young people? Don't ever use the words "you always," "you shouldn't," or "you never," and complaining is a *NO.* I'm living proof! Married, happily, for fifty-eight years.

—**HELEN CARLSON,** born October 11, 1919, is a retired commercial illustrator and real estate agent.

∾

"The Mature View"

The ages past so nobly aid our sense.
I've learned appreciation's at the core.
My heritage immersed in reverence;
the precious gifts from all who've gone before.
So many lives have left their legacy;
all human progress there for all to share.
'though free to all, I think it just for me.

My focus now finds "fair" to trump "despair";
I've tamed that urge fore'er demanding more.
Afflicted not by youth's untamed desires,
discern'd and learn'd what waits beyond the door,
I'll master now to tame ambition's fires.
The man who sees the glass half full is wise.
But youth, demanding it be full, brings sighs.

—**RONALD JONES,** born November 17, 1932, is a
retired environmental consultant to industry.

∾

$\mathcal{T}$he only good thing about being over sixty-five
that I particularly embrace is Viagra! It puts us
on a level playing field with the thirty-year-olds, and
they should hold their wives and girlfriends close
because we are armed and dangerous!

—**ROBERT CONRAD,** born March 1, 1935, is a
television and film actor perhaps best known for his work in
The Wild, Wild West in the 1960s.

∾

$\mathcal{H}$ave you heard the expression "Old age is not
for sissies"? Well, it's true in a lot of aspects
when you get to my age of eighty-eight.

In my last year at Berkeley High, I was captain
of the football team and had a very serious injury
to my right knee during the last game. I was told I
would never walk again, but through exercise and

perseverance, I survived! In 1936 I opened my first Physical Culture Studio, although I went to Chiropractic College, studied *Gray's Anatomy* cover to cover, I was ridiculed and made fun of. I was a runt, a crackpot, and charlatan because I was charging money for people to get in shape. Yesterday I was a liar and a cheat, today I'm an authority and I survived! I went through World War II in the South Pacific, Guadalcanal, and Suva—I survived! At sixty I towed a 1,000-pound boat from Alcatraz to Fisherman's Wharf in San Francisco, handcuffed and feet shackled. At seventy, I towed seventy people in seventy boats a mile and a half in Long Beach Harbor, handcuffed and feet shackled—I survived! I was told that I would never last on television—I survived for thirty-four years! The great thing is that I never gave up and I was able to reap the rewards of my perseverance.

Aging is like a sport, you have to work at living longer. The beautiful thing is that if we keep in shape and we have our physical and mental faculties about us, then we're going to enjoy old age. We can appreciate the fact that we're alive and living to enjoy them. Many people complain about their aches and pains but have to learn to live with them. To live life to the fullest, normalize your weight and watch your diet—it could add years to your life. Today, the medical profession takes people who are seventy, eighty, and ninety years of age, and doubles their strength and endurance with a program of systematic exercise. Old age is heaven on earth and a blessing if you're in shape. If you're not in shape, it can be "hell on earth." I'm very fortunate that I have been in my profession and enjoying my old age because I have practiced what I preached all these years. I believe that anything in life is possible if you can make it happen! Oh yes, one more thing, I can't afford to die—it will wreck my image!

—JACK LA LANNE, born September 26, 1914, is a physical fitness guru and the host of television's *The Jack La Lanne Show,* which ran for twenty years.

∿

*B*est things about being sixty-eight years old:

1. We do not have any anxiety on Sunday about Monday morning work, although we liked our jobs. This is all "in the mind stuff" but it no longer exists when you can sleep till 7:30 A.M. at *the earliest!*

2. One can travel more and do it when you want in the off-season.

3. One can walk away from most anything one does not enjoy. There is no one that one has

to impress by "being there"—to the end.

4. You can take up new endeavors that *you* enjoy. Like visiting every beach in North Carolina at your leisure.

5. In North Carolina for most of the year you only have to put on a T-shirt and shorts. It takes forty-three seconds to get dressed. Plus shaving can be decreased in volume per week.

6. There is a lot of older bonding, thank God. We are nice to our peers and understand one another.

7. You can catch up on your reading. Book clubs are very popular and stimulating.

8. You can go to the gym at 1:00 P.M. when there is not a crowd. *Very important to me.* One hour three times a week.

9. We gave our second car to a daughter nine years ago and have managed well without one. This cuts down worry and repair time.

10. One can go to daytime sporting events, e.g., college baseball at UNCW here in Wilmington, North Carolina.

—**HUGH VAN ZELM,** born December 15, 1933, worked for more than thirty years for an electronics company as a personnel manager, then became a corporate equal employment manager; he is married with two daughters and one grandson.

∼

I just love being sixty-eight. It's the best age there is. In three months sixty-nine will be the best age, provided the good Lord lets me see it.

It seems to me that happiness is appreciating what we have. By now I have found out that a lot of things didn't matter anyway, especially after the top layer of pride is erased. It's not so bad to admit it when I make a mistake.

Amazing how few people I need to impress anymore. If people want to be wrong, they don't have to listen to me; I might not know anyway. It's easy to say I just forgot that, even though I never knew. Sometimes there isn't a fine line between the two. "The Senior Moment" idea comes in handy also.

After all, since life is a gift from God, I need to do my part by keeping my mind alert, my body in the best possible shape, and enjoy and make life a little easier for others. We are all in it together. It's wonderful at any age!

—**FRANCES QUESENBERRY**, born December 31, 1933, is a retired librarian.

∾

*T*he momentum of old age should expand the imagination to the point where myth becomes reality.

—**VIDAL SASSOON**, born January 17, 1928, is a celebrity hairstylist.

∾

*Y*es, it's true, folks, as you suspect, approaching your later years is a pain, a downer, a setback, to get to the deteriorating part of life, the "golden years." On the other hand, it is a joy and a privilege to make it to this point because, as we say so often, it sure does beat the alternative!

Here we are, toughing it out, and treasuring the toughness skills that brought us this far. We're seniors now and it's hard to do things that used to be easy, it's hard to walk, hard to carry things, hard to keep things organized. It's a nuisance that everything has to be a production, but that's what life with old age is. I've added MS to the mix, too, an extra challenge. I find that I have to rely on friends and family for many favors. But that's how it goes, and that's what I do.

I've been very lucky to live so long; I know dear ones who didn't have that good fortune. It's not good to have a serious debilitating disease; it is good that it progresses very slowly. Many are not so fortunate. It was disappointing to take early disability retirement; on the other hand, it was wonderful that there was such a thing and that Social Security disability and my long-term disability insurance were available when I needed them. It was wonderful indeed.

Because I have difficulty walking, I shopped, for years as it turned out, for a house with no steps to climb. I found a pretty little bungalow/cottage set up against a greenbelt, my own private arboretum, a nature lover's setting, perfect for me, a wonderfully comfortable place to be. So there's another plus!

Minuses and pluses, pluses and minuses, we never know when the next jolt may be, life's full of surprises. For me, three years ago, it was a new diagnosis, cancer this time, at a very teeny early stage discovered by a mammogram and excised within weeks, followed by radiation for seven weeks, now tamoxifen daily for five years. So here we are again, time for more philosophy as I realize that cancer, bad and scary for sure, is not as big a shadow in my life as is MS, a daily challenge of coping.

It's good to be at a time of life for having wisdom and friends, a fine family, and many interesting activities, with lots of ways to be useful in the world. It's fun to watch baseball on TV with grandsons, and to be wheeled to our Easter picnic in the arboretum. It's terrific to have kids, grandkids, friends and their friends, stop by for Sunday soup (or salad) as desired; I enjoy the get-together. It's a pleasure to get to yoga and water exercise and feel the power and strength that come with physical movement; I'm glad to be a part of that.

I have a small job and I serve on a board; I find special delight in sharing the energy and momentum of intergenerational programs, too, both computer-pal correspondence and a marvelous senior/youth partnership with a co-op school and senior activity center over in the university district.

All in all, my schedule's packed to the brim. I have fun at what I do, I live in a handsome corner of a beautiful city, and, despite MS and cancer and advancing years, I thrive, thrive, thrive.

—**RANDI RYAN,** born June 4, 1935, is a retired educator and child nutrition program administrator and now writes.

> None are so old as those who have
> outlived enthusiasm.
> —HENRY DAVID THOREAU

*M*y zest for life has more to do with my positive approach than the number of years I have lived.

Be limber in body and mind. Exercise regularly and be open and receptive to new ideas. Relax and flow with change instead of resisting.

Love yourself—develop self-esteem. You are the "star" in your life's drama. Take the first steps in extending love, understanding, and forgiveness as we live by the "golden rule."

Surprise yourself! Life is never boring if you are just a little loony. Give life a light touch. Don't be too serious—life is too mysterious.

Therefore, I'm limber, loving, and just a little loony!

—LUCILLE C. JONES, born January 17, 1914, worked for Sears.

*A*ging means you're alive. We don't have to talk about aging, it's happening.

It's a great time to eat less and feel sexy. This is a no-brainer what with the shrinking economy. Feeling sexy is a challenge. Figuring out how to is one way to fight off Alzheimer's.

I, Jerry, encourage everyone to swim. In addition to it being good for the cardiovascular system and minimizing stress on the kneecaps, it's great for the mind. In a previous life we were all swimming in Mommy's tummy. The ocean or the pool is the closest we can return to the time when everything was given to us unconditionally. They were probably the best nine months of our lives.

When I'm below sea level I'm back in the womb living the good life. Just make sure you can swim and come up for air once in a while. Otherwise you'll drown.

To the young people: Question everyone who thinks they have the answers and listen to your inner voice.

—**JERRY STILLER,** born June 8, 1927, and **ANNE MEARA,** born September 20, 1929, are the comedy duo Stiller and Meara as well as husband and wife. Jerry Stiller has starred as Frank Costanza, George's father, on *Seinfeld*, and currently appears as Arthur Spooner on *The King of Queens*; Anne Meara has earned acclaim for her work in the theater, including a 1993 Tony nomination as Best Featured Actress in a Play for her performance in Eugene O'Neill's *Anna Christie*.

∽

"Full Circle"

I was a child.
The world was fresh and new
and full of mystery.
Why do the birds fly?
Why does the stream flow downhill?
Where does the sun hide in the night,
the moon in the day?
Oh, the wonder of the world!

Then I grew up.
I had no time
for the birds or the stream,
the sun or the moon.
I had to earn a living,
keep abreast of the next man.

Now I'm old.
I watch the birds
soar in the sky,
watch the streams
ripple through the woods.
I bask in the warmth of the sun,
delight in the glow of the moon.
Oh, the wonder of the world!

—JUDY DAVEY, born December 16, 1921, is a retired
tailor who now writes.

～

*M*y recipe for aging into a good, healthy long life is to eat well-balanced meals and try to develop the "—tion" habit: Education, Digestion, Recreation, Stimulation, Elimination, and Meditation.

What we are is God's gift to us. What we become is our gift to God.

Develop hobbies so you can prepare for a holistic retirement. Forty is the old age of youth, fifty is the youth of old age. Get a good education and prepare and think of what you want to do with the rest of your life.

Don't make rash decisions; look before you leap.

We are creatures of habit, therefore live every day to its fullest as if you will die tomorrow, but plan for the future as if you will live forever. Learn to say no when necessary, and when you say yes, say it wholeheartedly.

Whatever you earn, save a portion and don't spend more than you earn. Stay away from smoking, and drink in moderation. Most important for staying healthy is to exercise regularly and keep developing healthy habits to pursue your dreams. Always plan ahead. Patience is a virtue, for life has a lot to offer, such as ambition, inspiration, perspiration, self-control, and discipline along with some luck.

These ingredients enable one to grow older gracefully, peacefully, with good health and contentment. Remember that aging is natural, as it depends on heredity, physical health, mental health, and nutrition.

Enjoy your years.

—**JACK BURGEMAN,** born May 28, 1923, is a World War II veteran who later owned a medical collection agency and also worked for the state of Illinois collecting unpaid student loans.

∽

The best part of growing older is that at least one can become real and true friends with men—all kinds of men, young, old, and in between, hunks and dweebs, whatever. Sex doesn't enter into it and sometimes for the first time in your life you will really have a rewarding experience not tainted by the attraction of that nature.

You can also flirt all you like since you've become harmless. This is lots of fun and most men respond well.

I think the joy is in losing certain inhibitions of the above nature and the "trying to please" nature and just being able to say and do pretty much what pleases you. I will be nearly eighty by the time this book comes out, and I must say I am looking forward to that milestone immensely.

—**LIZ SMITH,** born December 11, 1925, has written a gossip column for the New York *Daily News, Newsday,* and the *New York Post.*

~

I am:

Happier than I was at 65.

Healthier than I was at 60.

More focused than I was at 50.

More at peace than I was at 40.

More contented than I was at 30.

Wiser than I was at 20.

For all of this, I am eternally grateful to my God, my wife, my children, my parents and grandparents, friends, and all the people and forces that have inspired and influenced me through the years.

Why?

I am happier than I was at sixty-five because of the successful transition from being primarily dedicated to my profession to being primarily dedicated to living in harmony with nature and society.

I am healthier than I was at sixty because I am learning the art of pursuing total wellness. I know that physical, mental, and spiritual wellness cannot be separated, and that I am in control of my wellness. I am grateful for the input of health professionals, psychology and sociology professionals, and spiritual leaders, but I know that my total wellness is my responsibility.

I am more focused than I was at fifty because I am more dedicated to living in harmony with nature and my fellow man. I know that we depend on one another, that cooperation transcends competition, and that the art of listening, learning, communicating, and understanding is essential to universal harmony with nature and society.

I have more peace of mind than I did at forty because I have learned and practiced the art of prayerful meditation and living each moment. Peace of mind comes with understanding that the past cannot be changed, and my only influence on the future will result from living the present moment successfully.

I am more contented than I was at thirty because my expectations are more realistic. Today, I am better able to gratefully accept the opportunities that come my way and derive satisfaction from engaging in the useful and simple activities, rather than the spectacular.

I am wiser than I was at twenty because of all of the above, and the knowledge that there is so much yet to learn and so many opportunities to serve and participate in what life has to offer.

—J. T. HUNDLEY, born February 24, 1928, is a retired marketing specialist and business systems developer.

∾

*I*n my cartoons the children are between eighteen months and seven years old. Hanging out with that group for decades has kept me from aging. I'm one of those people who think young. And I don't even drink Pepsi!

The ideas for my 365 cartoons each year flow more easily at eighty than they did at twenty-five. I've lived through it all. If I repeat a gag from long ago, I just claim memory loss.

Family Circus © Bil Keane 2002.

At cartoonists' gatherings the gang now looks at me intently when I'm speaking. My wife says it's because I drool. Anyhow, it's gratifying to get respect from a crowd some of whom make their living being the most disrespectful people on earth.

For you young people starting out, this is the most important commandment to remember: Thou shalt honor thy elderly.

—**BIL KEANE**, born October 5, 1922, created the comic strip "The Family Circus" in 1960, which now appears in more than 1,500 newspapers, making it the most widely syndicated cartoon panel in America.

I really enjoy saying "I'm a senior citizen" to the ticket sellers at movies. I enjoy those discounts. However, before I got remarried a few years ago, I always presumed that most ladies did not want me to ask their age when I went on a first date. While at a movie with a date one night, I asked for two "senior" tickets. Was that the wrong statement to make! My escort didn't talk to me all during the movie; and when we parted, all she said was "You're very presumptuous." The only wisdom I can impart is keep your date far enough away from the ticket booth, so she can't hear you asking for senior discounts.

—THOMAS M. WHALING, born June 9, 1933, is an attorney.

~

I believe what I have learned the most after retiring is that having friends is one of the most valuable assets in this life. And following that is the ability to laugh, especially at yourself. Be kind, be considerate, be thoughtful of others, and be patient (although this is extremely difficult to do at times)! So many people in this world are under the assumption that attending the house of worship of their choice (whether it be Catholic, Methodist, Jewish, or any other religion) every week entitles them to call themselves "good religious" people. They do not realize that if in their everyday lives they do not show kindness, help others, say hello, hold the door open for someone, and just be considerate of others, then their going to sit in their house of worship does not make them a "good religious" person any more than going and sitting in the garage makes them a car!

—**ELIZABETH STRASSER,** born May 17, 1937, is a retired data input operator and currently involved in volunteer work and music organizations.

∽

𝓕or me, one of the joys of being over sixty-five is that people have stopped trying to sell you life insurance. Another is the growing number of issues, in the newspapers and elsewhere, that you no longer give a damn about. Your hormones have stopped jerking you around, though there is still a twinge now and then. And you've long since stopped keeping track of the top forty pop song hits. Also, in public, people don't get alarmed seeing you talk to yourself, or wearing one black shoe and one brown. In fact, people don't expect anything much of you at all. And that's a relief.

—**JOHN UPDIKE,** born March 18, 1932, is an author and two-time winner of the Pulitzer Prize.

∽

$\mathcal{I}$'m 100 years old. It doesn't seem possible. At times it seems long and other times it seems short. I was born in Jamaica, New York, on July 30, 1902. I was married in 1921 and moved to New Jersey. My husband, Carl, and I raised two beautiful and talented daughters. I consider that my greatest achievement. I became a widow at age fifty-four. I'm a breast cancer survivor. I've been through some hard times, but I've kept in mind that "this too shall pass." I love God, and that has kept me going. I have seven grandchildren, twenty great-grandchildren, and one great-great-grandchild. They too keep me going.

I took up painting with pastels at age seventy and thoroughly enjoyed it. I sent one of my pastels to Mrs. Nixon and one to Mrs. Ford. They both sent me letters of appreciation. In 1992, at age ninety, I began writing short stories and children's books. Altogether I have written twenty-four books, all of which I self-published. My first one, *Angel #9*, was popular and many copies were sold. My next book, *Letters to Adrienne*, was written to my granddaughter. Adrienne was diagnosed with leukemia as a very young child. She kept her teddy bear by her side through everything, in and out of the hospital, through operations and long stays at Memorial Sloan-Kettering. On one of her trips through Penn Station, she lost Teddy! I began writing letters to

Adrienne from Teddy in Teddy Land. The collection became *Letters to Adrienne*. I am thankful that Adrienne is now a healthy, beautiful ten-year-old.

I've enjoyed writing; it's kept me busy. Keeping busy has been an important part of my life. Outside of my family life, I've belonged to church groups and women's clubs and I still play a pretty good game of bridge. I started the Historical Society in Ocean Grove, New Jersey, in 1969, and was in charge of furnishing an old Ocean Grove cottage, which is open to the public.

I've traveled throughout the United States and Canada. I have been to Europe and the British Isles many times. I've been to the Orient twice and cruised to South America, the Caribbean, and the Panama Canal. One of my favorites was a four-month trip on a Norwegian freighter.

It's been a wonderful life, and I've been truly blessed.

—**EDITH H. ASCHENBACH,** born July 30, 1902, is a retired housewife.

∽

I am a queen—although I wasn't born into royalty. My coronation took place as I stood transfixed over the incubator that held my first grandchild, a beautiful, fragile baby boy. Overnight, my son, Bill, and his beautiful wife, Marie, had made me Grandma Jayne. "Grandma?" I puzzled at the word. Shouldn't I feel suddenly older, certainly less glamorous? No, not for a second. Somehow I felt grander, the matriarch of a family made royal by the wonder of my beautiful grandchild. That was seventeen years ago and today that little preemie, Bradley Allen, a Brad Pitt lookalike, is a strapping six foot three pitcher on his high school baseball team and my devoted friend.

Two years later, Robert Edward, a clone of his beloved grandpa Steve, arrived. Bobby, a gifted musician with the brilliant and spontaneous wit of his grandfather, became another loving heir to our dynasty.

And then eight years ago, our prayers were answered when Princess Amanda danced into our lives. Forever whirling and twirling, giggling or singing, this blonde angel was the apple of Grandpa's eye. Even watching her sleep brings joy to my heart.

Recently eight of my step-grandchildren by Dr. Steve Allen, Jr., and his brother, Brian, paid me a visit. When it came time to return home, three of these darling grandsons asked if they could stay and live with me. "Merciful heavens, why ever would you want to do that?" I asked. "Because you make us feel so good, Grandma," they assured me, warming my heart. The truth is, each of my eleven grandchildren makes *me* feel special.

Our beloved grandpa Steve is gone now, but life is for the living and I live happily with and for these best friends who keep me young. Nothing compares to the hugs and kisses, whispered secrets, and genuine "I love you, Grandma's" from our own flesh and blood. It makes getting older, arthritis or not, the prime period of life.

Recently as I was leaving a star-studded party through a poorly lit tunnel on the former Harold Lloyd estate, a young man whom I had never met stepped forward, graciously took my arm, and escorted me down the steep staircase. It was the divine George Clooney, and for one magical moment I was indeed a queen—what a fringe benefit to getting older.

But, oh, I almost forgot senior citizen discounts—they're nice, too.

—**JAYNE MEADOWS,** born September 27, 1924, acted in movies and on television and is best known as one-half of the comic duo with her late husband, Steve Allen.

～

*T*oday, on my eightieth birthday, as I sat down at my computer and received an uplifting, fun birthday message from one of my grandchildren—

an extremely busy, second-year medical student at the University of South Carolina—I immediately thought of two things that keep me feeling much younger than my years:

1. Learning something new at every opportunity (this computer has given me so much enjoyment and entertainment).

2. Taking every opportunity to laugh—and looking for more opportunities.

—**MARIGRACE BALDWIN,** born August 21, 1922, was a full-time homemaker who raised five children and was later an office worker and accountant.

∽

To the younger generation I might offer a tip and also a warning. As a child I spent much of my time with my elders and found it fascinating to listen to their life experiences. It was like entering a world of romance and fiction, but it wasn't fiction, it was true life. I also had the joy of sharing it with other people who actually went through the experiences. You'd better take advantage of these opportunities now, and you'll never say to yourself in years to come, "I wish I'd asked so-and-so about such-and-such." By then it may be too late. On the other side of the coin, I have often mentioned regarding the evolution of my career as a thought-reader and mentalist that I envisioned doing this as early as five years old and it was one of the blessings of my life because I had committed myself early enough that no one had a chance to teach me that the things I would eventually develop could not be done.

This, however, can be counterbalanced by advantages I see as years have gone by, bringing me into my late sixties. There is the absolute joy of being cantankerous. I always envied my elders, as they were able to get away with murder in what they said. I recall watching guests flow by on the Jack Parr, Steve Allen, and Johnny Carson shows who left me filled with admiration. What came out of their mouths could just not be said by younger people, as the remarks would have seemed just plain inappropriate. But they never seemed tasteless from an older person because somehow it was obvious that they were couched and expressed with wisdom. In a way, older people can get away with just as much as young kids who on Art Linkletter's *People Are Funny* used to say "the darndest things."

I also recall a commonly spoken line through the years by the great personalities within the arts, science, or politics. They were responding to the question: "If they had their life to live over again, would they have changed anything?" With apparent wisdom the inevitable answer would be no. Even as a child I would become annoyed with that response, as how could anyone not change actions of the past if they had the wisdom of reflecting on life's experiences. Consequently, my answer to that same question is simply, "You're damn right I would."

Simply having the richness of experiences to build upon, it is obvious I would not have said the same things or handled them in the same way or trusted the same people or mistrusted others. Can I share with you an example? I hope this reader does not consider me imbecilic, stupid, or naïve, but I admit to you that there was actually a time in my life where I honestly felt that attorneys could be trusted! If that were not enough, I honestly believed that there were honest politicians!

Furthermore, in the earlier days of my career when I was doing the Joey Bishop nighttime television show on the ABC network, and spending an awful lot of time in the Hollywood area, I thought that Hollywood was a glamorous place. But even then, though age had not taught me such, I had an intuition that it would be the last place on earth I'd want to live. I don't feel that way anymore now that Afghanistan has come into the picture!

In the early days, while traveling throughout the country developing my career, I was still attending a university. We had been taught from most of the psychology books from the past that reiterated that our unconscious was like a film negative with our life experiences impressed upon it. Furthermore, under certain conditions these "forgotten" life experiences could be recalled whether it be with hypnosis or what have you. In recent years it has become clear that such is absolutely not the case. We do not have memories of our entire lives embedded in our unconscious mind. Instead, as time goes by and we evolve with more experiences, we remember the past in a different way. It is perhaps for this reason that as the years go by we often remember best those most delectable things in our lives, and if they weren't so delectable, they seemed to have a better taste as our memories alter them. I would suggest that such changes of memory start to take place as early as the late teens and early twenties.

But I think one of the choicest advantages of growing older is that of realization. You become more selective in your illusions and delusions. A perfect example is the realization that the person who points out that he has hundreds and hundreds of friends is generally an extraordinarily lonely person. But true wisdom is in realizing that if you can count your true friends on the fingers of one hand, you have richness beyond any jewelry. Indeed, if you include all five fingers you may be naïvely inaccurate in your appraisal of who your true friends really are.

In conclusion, while one may not as the years go by hear as sharply and see as clearly or walk as rapidly, somehow the one quality that seems to become stronger is that of taste. For one inevitably savors life with a greater delectability, and as I have said many times, "It is the choice of savoring every day of one's life—after all, this is not a rehearsal."

—**THE AMAZING KRESKIN,** born January 12, 1935, is a mentalist and magician whose show, *The Amazing World of Kreskin,* aired in the 1970s, and he remains a frequent guest on television and radio.

∾

*A*mong the advantages of being older and retired are the freedom to say what we think without fear of affecting our careers or place in society and for those of us who are able, to give freely of our time, wisdom born of experience, and the skills of our trade or profession without consideration of recompense but solely for the joy of helping others.

—**HOWARD D. HARRISON, M.D.,** Governing Committee-Senior Physicians Group, A.M.A., born June 18, 1930, is a retired doctor.

∾

1. The competition is over. You can relax. You've made your life what it is and you no longer need to prove yourself. You can

relax and enjoy whatever degree of involvement you want.

2. You can take a longer-term, more detached perspective. In so doing you may be able to continue to contribute to your old field of work or to a new field of interest. You may be able to give useful advice to those coming along behind you. It is rewarding to feel that you are helping others.

3. You can take more time for friends and family. You realize that all along they have been what counts most. It's not fame, glory, position, or money that is important. It is what you do for others in your relationships with them and now you can concentrate on that more.

—**ADMIRAL STANSFIELD TURNER,** born December 1, 1923, is the former director of the Central Intelligence Agency.

～

*A*n unmistakable fact of everyone's life is that it's going to end. So what more can anyone wish for than that it end at a good place? For me, personally, I can think of no better place than at my desk in my office at *60 Minutes*, where I've spent a good part of the last thirty-five of eighty glorious years on this planet. However, for the time being, I have no plans to go anywhere. Try me again in twenty years.

—**DON HEWITT,** born December 14, 1922, is creator and executive producer of *60 Minutes*.

**Wrinkles should merely indicate where
the smiles have been.**
—M<small>ARK</small> T<small>WAIN</small>

I am a retired neurologist from Russia. Now I study English in English as a second language classes. To improve my English I attend a writing class with writer Bea Mitz. She encouraged me to write compositions and even poetry. As a result I've written an autobiographical book about Russian Jews. This occupied my mind and my life became more interesting.

I wonder that in my age my senses became some-how more poignant. It seems that I am always in a hurry to catch everything that was lost during my lifetime. There's so much I didn't accomplish—if not now, when?

In everything I want to find the essence of the

days that passed, the core, the reasons of what happened, to be more prepared to live, to think, to love, and even be creative. Yes, I still need to get to the roots of things.

Because of it, being eager to know what is going on in our community, I attended—don't fall from your chair—classes at the police academy. The excitement of that unusual experience in my life inspired me to write a poem. Here it is:

"Police Academy"

Don't laugh at me,
I'm taking classes at the police academy.
Imagine me in my seventies
Still eager to fulfill my life motto: "Not to miss."

I've learned about domestic violence and crime,
I admire policemen who sacrifice their lifetime.
I've seen smart dogs searching for drugs,
They are trained by professional cops.

For the first time I shot
From a real gun, but it isn't good,
I'm excited, in vain I try to hit the target
As I'm taught by a shooting sergeant.

It is important to know that policemen have to fight
With a diversity of things that aren't right.
I feel compassion for you, who daily risk your lives,
I understand the anxious waiting of your children and
   wives.
God bless you!

—**SOFIA GELMAN,** born December 30, 1930, was chief
neurologist of the city of Batumi, Georgia, Caucasus, in the
former U.S.S.R. and has written an autobiography and
published poetry.

∾

*M*emory gratifies. Time is a grand vintner, bot-
tling up memories in your cerebral cellars to
be mellowed with time, later decanted to the next
generation. I have been blessed with a rich life during
which I have met presidents, kings, racing drivers,
jocks, and just about every other imaginable sort of
celebrity. I am often asked to recall those encounters—and in the spirit of expanding the bounds of
good taste, I often do. Who would have dreamed
that the Eisenhower years or even the swingin' '60s
would become so interesting to a generation that
never lived through them? And who would have
dreamed that I would get so much pleasure out of
telling them about it?

Personally, the greatest thing about getting

older is being here to enjoy it. That may seem profoundly obvious at first glance, but consider the longevity of my peers—the so-called glamour girls from decades past: Thelma Todd, Jean Harlow, Carole Lombard, Frances Farmer, Carole Landis, Veronica Lake, Marilyn Monroe, Betty Grable, Joi Lansing, Cleo Moore, Jayne Mansfield, Barbara Ruick, Leigh Snowdon, Barbara Nichols, Barbara Peyton, Marilyn Maxwell, Marie McDonald, Marie Wilson, Diana Dors, Sharon Tate, Inger Stevens, and Dorothy Stratten were all, in varying degrees, famous, blonde, beautiful, and billed as sex goddesses of their respective eras. Most of them did not live to see fifty-five. Our profession is perhaps the most competitive in the world.

For, to be glamorous, to be beautiful, is to be doomed eventually to be disappointed. As my friend the late Dorothy Lamour, one of the most glamorous women I have ever known, once said, "Time keeps rollin' on." She shrugged. "What're you going to do?" Answer: Get as old as you can. It's essential.

Whether or not you make your living being beautiful, the longer you live, the more you recognize that special something deep inside all of us that radiates beauty. Regardless of the outside of you, the beauty inside you will never change, for as long as you live.

Shine that beauty on someone else. Time passes quickly and it is the best way to leave your mark. In the memory of others is true immortality.

—**MAMIE VAN DOREN,** born February 6, 1931, is a singer and actress.

~

*O*f course, for the purist, the following transgression might be described as immoral, perhaps illegal. Still, this crime deserves to be defined in a context where the gatekeepers of morality are less than austere.

The act has an aura of sin, but even the most inflexible proponents of goodness will have to concede that it is of the venial category.

Consider: What is unusual about the piling on of more strawberries in their pint basket than it is designed to hold?

These arc-shaped ladies, with their canes and walkers lain aside, perform this little thievery so openly that the process takes on a kind of naturalness, perhaps even innocence.

Besides, what other temptations are really comparable to this luscious fruit, now, in the sunset of our autumnal years.

Despite the inexorable laws of physics, which cause the added berries to teeter on the brink of falling, these beehive-coiffed harpies manage to insert the totality into the confines of a plastic bag with practiced dexterity.

Nevertheless, the appearance of artlessness persists even under the quizzical stare of the cashier at the suspiciously bulging package. He makes no vocal interposition.

Besides, of all the virtues, the greatest one is charity. It is the Paschal season, the ultimate time for forgiveness; these are, after all, our golden years.

—**CONSTANTIN GOCHIS,** born March 16, 1918, is a retired lieutenant colonel of the U.S. Army and was director of a large New York City agency.

∽

From the vantage point of eighty-five plus years, I can say that one wakes up every morning realizing that just being there is another victory. My arteries are hard enough so that I don't have migraine headaches anymore. My spine is pretty well ankylosed with osteoarthritis and that means I don't have low back pain anymore. Friends seem more precious than they used to because there are fewer of them, as age or dementia makes inroads into my peers of my own age. I have learned at eighty-five you can still do two full-time jobs, and as a matter of fact, I think the reason I can say this at eighty-five is that I have never stopped working, and working hard, and trying to make a difference.

—**C. EVERETT KOOP, M.D., Sc.D.,** born October 14, 1926, was U.S. Surgeon General from 1981 to 1989.

∾

*M*y daughter-in-law, Helen, turned forty. Much to my surprise, she tells me she feels old. That started me thinking about my seventy-four years of life.

I am a survivor of the Holocaust. As a teenager, I was put in a concentration camp. Never did I think about getting old, getting married, having children or grandchildren or great-grandchildren. I never expected to survive.

Today I am blessed with a husband, children, grandchildren, and great-grandchildren.

I realize the years don't stop. Time advances and I don't feel much different as I age. My state of mind accepts the inevitable changes in my physical structure. Of course, I have a few pains here and there, but that goes with the territory. Long ago, I learned that complaining doesn't help alleviate distress.

So I tell Helen, "Enjoy your surroundings. People like to see smiles, kindness, and chances are you'll get the same in return. Day by day, try to take things in stride and enjoy every minute." I take Helen's hand. "Don't think about your age. You will be fine if you take it easy. Furthermore, in my eyes you are still young."

Helen smiles and gives me a big hug.

—**LOLA SASSOVER,** born October 19, 1928, is the mother of two children, the grandmother of fourteen, and worked in her husband's business.

∾

As I think about writing you to tell you how it feels to be seventy-something, I am sitting on the deck of my home on the shores of Lake Tahoe. It's about noon on a beautiful summer day. The skies are blue, the lake is bluer, with a light breeze ruffling the surface and making it a pleasure for both the sailors and the water-skiers gliding across the sparkling waters. The sight of this gives me a pleasant sense of well-being, partly because I can sit here and enjoy it as long as I like. I didn't have to go to work this morning to a job I disliked, and I won't have to tomorrow or the next day or the next. In fact, I am about to pour myself a cold martini, followed by a nice lunch to be followed by a siesta. If all this sounds idyllic, it is.

But I am able to enjoy it most because I have the sense of having earned it. All those fifty-some years in the entertainment business (continuing some to this day) doing the things I loved doing best—earning a living by performing for people all over the world. I'll never forget those years of early calls, long shooting days, and late shooting nights. Now those memories are sweet and mellow in my mind as I remember all the wonderful actors, directors, writers, crews, etc., I have performed with. And most of all, the beautiful girl who has been by my side for these fifty-two years. She's seen me in both triumph and disaster, and when things were good, and kicked me in the pants when I was down and said, "Get up and get 'em again, Tiger."

So, all these memories wander through my mind now and I thank God and good fortune for my blessings. There are many things I think about ... humanity, life, the state of the world, but I'm afraid those will have to wait for another letter, Willard. I think my lunchtime martini is about ready. Join me?

—**PETER GRAVES,** born March 18, 1926, is an actor who starred in *Mission: Impossible* and *Airplane!*

∾

I write as one who has been "refired" (the word "retired" is not in my vocabulary) for eleven years, and I am enjoying this exciting new life. Although one cannot deny the inevitable losses and issues of growing older, aging *is* a matter of the mind. I like what Chief Justice Oliver Holmes once wrote to Julia Powers: "I am glad you are seventy years old. I say glad, for it is better to be seventy years young, than forty years old!" We may grow older, but never be old.

What wisdom would I pass on to younger generations? *Find a new vocation.* The joy of "retirement" is that work does not get in the way of life. We are free to devote ourselves to what really matters to us. We can make a difference! Aging is a time to give back to the world our gifts of time and talents. We must never surrender to the cliché that older people have no worth or value. We can be just as active as our health allows.

It is a time to shine. Someone has quipped that the three great temptations of old age are: to whine, decline, or recline. Doubtless to say, there are some older people who fall into those categories. But my experience has been that many older people *shine* with a contagious optimism and a creative spirit that becomes a role model for all generations. Beautiful young people are accidents of nature; beautiful older people are works of art.

Continue growing. Carl Jung said it well: "We cannot live the afternoon of life according to the program of life's morning." Medical science has given us bonus years to live, and the "retirement life" can be a time for growth as a person. Freed from the obligations and demands of the workaday world, we now have time to grow our souls and discover the inner strength that comes from the contemplative life.

I truly believe there is a "new elder" emerging in our society, who goes beyond the boundaries and images of aging, creating new models of what we can be in our later years. This has been the passion of my "refired" life. As the Japanese say, "The sunsets of life are as glorious as the sunrises."

So they are.

—DR. RICHARD L. MORGAN, born March 7, 1929, is the author of *No Wrinkles On The Soul; I Never Found that Rocking Chair; Autumn Wisdom; Remembering Your Story;* and *The Bible Speaks to Third and Fourth Agers.*

∽

*O*ne of the great things about getting older (but what is old these days?) is that when your body starts falling apart, so does your eyesight, so when you look in the mirror in the morning, you still look pretty good. My advice is *don't get glasses.*

—ANDY WILLIAMS, born December 3, 1927, is a singer.

∽

*T*he secret of long life is not perfection, rather the ability to adapt.

This statement seems to epitomize for me the meaning of advancing one's later years. It is not the progress from ninety years to ninety-one but the

"Oh, so you wanna play rough, huh?"

matter by which I have approached that progression. It is my desire to live each day to the fullest; to give to others something of the good I find in each day; and to remember my mantra: "This is the day that the Lord hath made. Let us be glad and rejoice in it." [Psalm 118:24]

Because of the family heritage of good genes, on both sides of my family, my progress into aging seemed to be ordained. My parents each lived into their late nineties, as did many of my antecedents. My sister was ninety-nine. My mother was one of twelve cousins, nine of whom lived to be ninety-eight and one was 100. I adapted well to each decade until I, too, became a nonagenarian.

But from my parents and grandparents I inherited something far greater than worldly goods. This is the belief in our Heavenly Father who sent His Son so that we might learn to live better and to serve others. To His teachings I have tried to be true and thereby have received much joy and peace in my life.

I have had a good life, not always easy, but I have been blessed with good health, sight, and hearing, an alert mind. I have been able to adapt to changes in my lifestyle many times. And I am sure I have grown spiritually with each adaptation.

I am hoping to continue to believe I will live as

long as God has work for me to do on earth, and I will look forward to the transition when He is ready for me. I will adapt well then.

—JESSIE LOUISE DUNN, born November 3, 1910, was an academic dean of Marjorie Webster Junior College in Maryland.

∾

One of the great things about growing older is having grandchildren who will listen to your stories, such as:

A little old lady in New York took her dog out for a walk every night. As a good citizen she always obeyed the law that says: "Scoop up your dog's poop: Don't leave it sitting on the curb."

One evening as she and the dog were returning after their evening stroll, she had a small suitcase with her. She was walking close to the curb when a car slowed down beside her. An arm reached out and grabbed her suitcase. The car zoomed off into the city traffic.

And the little old lady laughed and laughed, just to think what the people in that car thought when they opened that suitcase and saw what was in it.

—PETE SEEGER, born May 3, 1919, is a musician and activist.

∾

I have lived over ninety years and would be glad to see more respect given by the general population to one another—courtesy by the driving public, in homes, schools, and the marketplace. A specific bit of advice I give to all is to treat others as you want to be treated. This makes life worthwhile.

"O'er the Hill"

Please, dear ones, as we have aged a bit,
As time allows we will,
Don't say in fun as many have done
That we are "o'er the hill."

For life is rich and blessings great,
There's time and zest though still,
We may not walk as fast as once—
"We're not yet o'er the hill."

Our hair will gray, our steps may falter,
Yet time will never kill
The memories of a pleasant life
Together are fulfilled.

—WILMA ROSE (CRUNKILTON) RACER, born June 12, 1912, is a full-time homemaker who has four children, eleven grandchildren, fifteen great-grandchildren, and one great-great-grandchild, and has been active for sixty years with the Ohio Extension Homemakers Council of Ohio State University as President and State Safety Chairwoman, among other roles.

~

O ld age can be a very liberating time of life. We have mostly come to terms with the physical slowing-down, both of the body and the workings of the mind. We are no longer responsible for every aspect of our children's lives; we no longer work to earn our living, nor do we have many of the house-keeping duties we once had.

Of course there is a downside, but that, too, we accept. We can deal with walking more slowly or tiring sooner. The spontaneous trips to the mall, the ability to travel on the spur of the moment, even the choices of nourishment are no longer limitless. We accept that we need to plan ahead, and are de-lighted with the activities offered to us.

We don't have to do the things we don't want to (well, maybe follow doctor's orders). Each day can be a new adventure, meeting new friends, enjoying the old, learning new things like quilting or Spanish, taking a walk in the great outdoors. We can indulge in quiet ac-tivities alone, like reading, meditation, or knitting.

You might say we are in our second childhood. We are watched over by others, fed, our illnesses checked on. If we are missing, someone will be there to see why or where. To some degree, we have be-come the child, and our children are the parents. And there is still the same love between us.

In my opinion, old age is the best of all possible worlds. I say the words of a prayer I learned long ago: "O Lord, support us all the day long, until the shadows lengthen and the evening comes, and the busy world is hushed, and the fever of life is over, and our work is done. Then in thy mercy grant us safe lodging, and a holy rest, and peace at the last. Amen."

—**NATALIE REID,** born September 25, 1918, taught French and hula in Hawaii and taught French in Illinois.

～

*W*hat I like best about getting old is that it certainly beats the alternative of not getting old. The trick is to be wise enough in your youth to exercise, eat properly, and maintain a positive attitude so you can enjoy your senior years.

—**WALLY AMOS,** born July 1, 1936, has been a theatrical agent, actor, television host, author, and is the creator of the Famous Amos Chocolate Chip Cookie Company.

～

*M*y wife and I are both eighty-two. We live in an institution dedicated to caring for older folks who need support in independent and assisted living. We just sold the only house we ever had; we lived in it for twenty-nine happy years and hoped we could live there until we died. However, man proposes, God disposes. Sickness made it mandatory that we sell our cherished domicile and we had to part with most of the things that had sentimental value.

After that sad introduction, how can I say it is great to be in old age? Easy. Think of the alternative. Life is beautiful and the love we have for each other and for so many of our relatives and friends warms our hearts. We feel that we are blessed to be alive and to be living with many older people who seem so sensitive to one another and who put themselves out to help in time of need. We are doubly blessed because we have so many relatives and friends who think of us and show their continuing love and respect for us.

How can we not rejoice in each new sunrise and celebrate each sunset? The gift of life and love makes us want to spend all of our time offering thanks for people who make up our world. We pray a lot for the poor countries and we hope that in the future the gap between the rich and the poor will become more narrow. I suppose the one thing we want more than anything else is peace in the world. Fear, hate, greed, and anger have had their day; now is the time to light some candles and stop cursing the darkness.

We don't really miss the house that much, and as for the things we thought we couldn't live without, we are doing just fine. Living in much smaller quarters makes it easier to find the things that we lose every morning and search for the rest of the day. There is some gremlin who takes things and puts them in the strangest places; luckily we have a twin gremlin who often puts them back. We now realize that small is beautiful.

When a friend cautioned me that I should be thinking of the hereafter at my age, I reassured him that I think of the hereafter at least twenty times a day. I go into one of our two rooms and ask myself, What am I here after?

Seriously, being old is full of surprises, not all of them are pleasant. We slowly lose the use of faculties, we lose our balance and often fall, but I wouldn't swap being old for anything in the world. Oh, what happy memories we have. I like that line— "Grow old along with me! The best is yet to be." My wife and I really believe that.

—JACK McCALL, born August 3, 1920, is a retired psychologist.

∾

For university professors, academic life involves both teaching and research. At some point one becomes a professor emeritus. Simply put, this means that you don't have to do anything and you don't get paid. You are retired from teaching, but there is no need to retire from doing research.

To oversimplify, one can divide a research career into three phases. In the first, you don't know enough to think conventionally. It isn't surprising that some of the great breakthroughs in science are made by researchers under thirty.

In the next phase you must read academic journals to know what has been done and what interesting problems await solution. This is the period dominated by the need to "publish or perish." Major contributions are made by many in this phase, along with a plethora of useful but incremental additions to existing knowledge.

The third phase usually begins when one reaches the certain age and becomes a professor emeritus. Freed from the necessity of publication, you can sit back, reflect, and ask big questions. Is the conventional wisdom in one's field fatally flawed? If so, should a new or highly revised approach be adopted? Or, if the core of current wisdom seems sound, has the field become encrusted with unnecessary technical material? If so, why not write *X for Dummies* with all the unnecessary baggage stripped away?

In the third phase of a career, a researcher can stand back, assess the situation, and think freshly. Armed with a lifetime of experience and knowledge, one can think big thoughts and approach one's field afresh. In many ways, this is the best of times.

—**WILLIAM F. SHARPE,** born June 16, 1934, won the Nobel Prize in Economic Sciences in 1990 and is Professor of Finance, Emeritus, Stanford University.

∿

*T*hank you for the invitation to share the fun of living to be in the eighth decade of life. God has blessed my life with adventure, that of serving in the U.S. Army Nurse Corps in France during World War II. This experience introduced an appetite to travel and I have learned "Blessed are the flexible, for they shall not be bent out of shape!" So numerous missionary itineraries have included the Philippines, Taiwan, Ecuador, Russia, Italy, and Belize, plus numerous American jaunts. God has also blessed me with the ability to see things funny and to see funny things.

Still on the go and loving every step of each mile!

—**VIOLET OLIVER,** born January 31, 1921, has been a registered nurse, a marketing director, a real estate broker, and owner and operator of a nursing home.

> I promise to keep on living as though I expected to live forever. Nobody grows old by merely living a number of years. People grow old only by deserting their ideals. Years may wrinkle the skin, but to give up interest wrinkles the soul.
> —Douglas MacArthur

I would like to say that one of my greatest joys was getting married at a very young age, having children, and seeing them grow to be adults with children of their own.

I now have four grandchildren and one great-grandchild; they are the focal point of my life. One can never realize the joy of children. Children are a source of daily learning.

The next greatest thrill of my life is to be married to the most wonderful woman in this hemisphere for forty-four years.

And finally to have served my country as a soldier in the U.S. Army for thirty years. As a child I always wanted to be a soldier; I fulfilled that childhood dream.

My advice to the present and upcoming generation would be to always respect your parents, love your country, and above all believe in the Almighty God and Jesus Christ. Make prayer a daily ritual within your life. And remember they live in the greatest country in the world.

Senior citizen and proud of it.

—**MELVIN MERRITT,** born November 26, 1936, is a retired military man of thirty years, the father of two children, the grandfather of four, and the great-grandfather of one.

∾

*I*t sounds simple, but we follow the golden rule, and treat people like we want to be treated. That goes for everybody, no matter who they are or what they do. After all, you catch more flies with sugar than you do with salt.

—**TOM CHRISTERSON,** born March 16, 1931, became the world's second recipient of the AbioCor implantable replacement heart on September 13, 2001, and **SPEEDY CHRISTERSON,** born August 8, 1931.

∾

*G*rowing up is serious business. As the years go by, we grow more and more serious, we may even become unbearable. Eventually, however, we come back to our childhood. We begin to live like eager little children as we learn to enjoy the day-to-day experiences of the moment. We no longer waste time in examining ourselves and others for flaws, but like little children we accept one another as we are. We live, once again, in the playgrounds of our youth. We do not see our scars as ugly, or our age as weakness. We know we are strong, we have survived.

The aerobic pools at the YMCA are great playgrounds. When we are in one of the exercise pools, we are on a level playing field. The water and its buoyancy make us the same size. We are talking heads. Treading water, the short ones and the tall ones chat away, trading stories, sometimes even listening to our hardworking aerobics teacher. We may have health problems but there's nothing wrong with our jaw muscles! So we discuss the latest fads in medicine, the wonders of our children and grandchildren, our latest operation—even the daily weather.

It makes no difference if accident or stroke has maimed. It makes no difference if a person is smart or dumb—some of the dumbest used to be the smartest, and we all know that. There is no sight quite like the courtesy and gentleness with which an old gentleman treats a young "special needs" woman. There is nothing sweeter than the smile he gets in return.

We relate to one another on a new level. Do we flirt? There comes a time when people collide, when skin touches skin. One lady really travels when she exercises and always manages to bump into a bearded gentleman who moves very slowly because of the aftermath of his stroke. She is always apologetic and flustered. I note, however, that it happens over and over and he makes little effort to avoid her. In fact, I think I caught the ghost of a smile on his face the other day, as he gave me a shy "thumbs-up" with his good hand! There is more than one way to make a connection, it seems.

My husband comes swimming with me. He has developed a new habit. He goes into the hot pool for the final ten minutes of the exercise hour. He says it helps to soothe his sore leg. I notice that a lot of ladies go into that pool also, and I can see a bit of gossip being bandied about in that steamy atmosphere! Of course, Bernie is not the only gaffer dallying in the steam, and it is true that I receive my share of second- and third-hand information from this activity. In fact, I wish my health would let me partake of both the steam and the conversation! It sounds like fun, and it can't be denied that there are several older gentlemen who look strangely fascinating in that other pool!

—**MARILYN TOLAN,** born October 31, 1921, is a retired computer systems analyst, mother of three, grandmother of six, and great-grandmother of two; and **BERNIE TOLAN,** born August 15, 1921, is a retired mathematics teacher; they have been married for nearly sixty years.

*M*y mantra is to always walk in the sunshine of life. As a former Olympic coach, consultant to the President's Council on Physical Fitness and Sports, founder of four New York State corporations, hall of famer, national speaker, author, teacher, etc., I sincerely believe that I have accomplished so much because of my *"I-can-do-it attitude."*

As a doctoral student at age seventy-one, I find my attitude is coming in handy, to say the least. Also all of my best and brightest seniors in my classes have the same attitude that age is just a number and "too bad the docs have to know what the number is."

—BETTY PERKINS-CARPENTER, born January 22, 1931, runs the website www.senior-fitness.com.

∾

*A*ll endings are sad, even the end of pregnancy. I resent my friends' wives who rob me of my friends, who end the meaning of this friendship. And all change too is sad, even a change for the better. Stars' meanings alter as we come near, but *we* never change really—though nothing stays truth in a third person's mouth.

What's new for the old is old for the new, so

how do we know where we are? I mean, the old are new yesterday, the young today. A child, not having been born, can't see this. Yet an old person feels newer today than yesterday when he was younger. So things get newer as they grow older, because today is younger than yesterday.

Old's the opposite of new, but also of young. Old people are more recently old than the unborn, more newly old, newer, constantly on the crest of the wave, advancing, nearer to that future from which the young are distant. Antiques grow ever newer— new hags, a new crone. Newborn babies are all wrinkled with age.

Last month is older than today. Is today younger, or only newer? The past, now old, was when the world was young. So we become younger and younger as we continue on and away from that old time when the world in flames was brand new, and so very aged it now seems. And we are newer, being more recent. . . . Memories of the future, the ancient future.

—**NED ROREM,** born October 23, 1923, is a composer, writer, and winner of a Pulitzer Prize.

∽

*O*ne great thing about getting old is retiring only after fourteen years of not retiring.

While employed, I enjoyed camping. So, we purchased an RV, recreational vehicle. We went camping alone and with our children.

Upon retiring from the workplace, we left the East Coast behind. For a time, we did what we wanted to and went camping where we wanted to, despite limited finances. Then we heard that the Army Corps of Engineers was hiring persons to man their entrance gates at their many campgrounds. Now, perhaps, we could do what we enjoyed and get paid for it. We prayed over each bid we made, and my wife received eighteen contracts in fourteen years, an unheard-of accomplishment. We traveled and camped from coast to coast with much enjoyment and meeting thousands of wonderful people, some with whom we are still in contact.

The wisdom we want to pass on to youngsters is: Don't make decisions for immediate satisfaction when they will have a negative impact in the future. Had we sat on the porch in retirement, we would have promptly wasted away. Our decision not to sit for those years resulted in enjoying fourteen years of not being retired after official retirement. All were years of active enjoyment and a contribution to the Corps of Engineers and the camping public. We made a lot of campers happy.

Now, at eighty years, I do mostly sit. My son says,

"Dad, at your age you are permitted to forget a few things and to sit on the porch."

—**TRUVAN T. GIBSON,** born July 2, 1922, retired from a career in marketing and spends his time primarily traveling by motor home; he has three children and seven grandchildren.

∽

The joys of reaching a certain age are many—the first minus is a little tear for all your pals who went on ahead.

My old foursome at Bel Air Country Club is down to just me—and I'm there putting too much.

My view of this situation in life is a black-and-white movie.

As far as music goes, when Basie went, it went.

However, I'm having a ball. About 200 pals showed up at my eightieth birthday party!

—**DICK MARTIN,** born January 30, 1922, is a performer perhaps best known for his work with Dan Rowan on *Rowan & Martin's Laugh-in.*

∽

In this long life of mine, what have I learned? I feel I have grown in compassion, in a deeper understanding of the meaning of love and loving, of detachment and gratitude. Still, there are rough edges that need to be smoothed: learning to listen more meaningfully, to better accept people as they are, and to never stop growing deeper and wiser and better able to be of service to others.

—**LOLA STONE,** born March 29, 1917, began painting and writing in her early teens, and along with her husband, Robert B. Stone, a noted author and lecturer, traveled to fifty-six countries around the world; they have two children.

∽

*A*fter twenty-six very good years in real estate, all of a sudden, at seventy-two years of age, I decided to be free. No open houses on Sunday, holidays without interruptions, visits to my grandchildren, and freedom to plan all of the above any way I wanted to do it, time to pursue hobbies like gardening, attend opera performances wherever and whenever I had the chance to go, attend classical music concerts, visit museums to enjoy art and study art history, that was on my agenda. But first I felt compelled to finally do some volunteer work. I simply did not have the time during my real estate career to do this other than volunteer in organizations within the real estate industry. Being a member of AARP, I received cards that suggested to fill them out if I would be willing to volunteer. Shortly after the mailing I was notified that I would be a member of the AARP Vote Committee. Great! Soon thereafter it was suggested to me to attend the Senior

Leadership class of Johnson County, which would introduce me to the many opportunities available to volunteer in our area. This course provided me with the best info possible. I was awed to find out how much volunteerism is practiced in this country. After careful consideration I decided to choose to be trained to become an LTC Volunteer Ombudsman. After several months of classes (once a week) I passed the test and was assigned to a nursing home close to where I live. At first the visits there were overwhelming. But soon I learned how much my visit meant to so many of the residents. After three years I still do my weekly visit, I look forward to the day I can schedule it into my busy weeks. I also volunteer at the Nelson-Atkins Museum of Art twice a month. Having volunteered there as a docent for seventeen years, I was still familiar with the museum and started at the information desk shortly after my retirement. The volunteer work keeps me focused to stay on a schedule but without any stress or pressure. I feel invigorated when I do it, and although I come home tired, it gives me a great deal of satisfaction to have spent my time in a meaningful way.

In between all this I manage to do my favorite things as mentioned above. I am well aware that together with everybody in this whole wide world I, too, get a year older every year, but so what? If I can keep doing what I elected to do for the last five years since my retirement, I am happy and content, and hope that someone reading this crazy story will lose the fear of "getting old." I miss my husband of forty-three years; he died of cancer ten years ago. But I know he would not like for me to sit at home and grieve his loss. Also, my children don't need to worry about me; as long as I have my health, I will keep busy. I never forget to be thankful that my husband brought me to this country fifty-four years ago. Coming home after each trip I take, I am more thankful and appreciative of all the opportunities this great country has to offer to everyone.

—**RUTH H. ILIFF,** born October 3, 1925, is a retired real estate broker.

∽

O ld age?—I'm only in it for the laughs.

—**LEON URIS,** born August 3, 1924, is a novelist.

∽

Y ou've heard the phrase "It's heck to get old, but it sure beats the alternative!" For some, retirement means inactivity; for my husband and me, it means freedom to do things! Bob retired from a life of diversified jobs at age sixty-five. Our five children were all on their own, the youngest being unmarried but living on campus while attending college. We'd sold our condo, bought a fifth-wheel trailer and truck, unloaded any possessions that would tie us down, and we "hit the road." We were free to stay wherever we stopped, or to move on to see more of our country. In the fifteen years that we continued to travel, we spent time in forty-eight states. On our fiftieth wedding anniversary we visited Hawaii. A future cruise may take us to Alaska. While one of our children was stationed with the Air Force in England, we visited twice and took time to see Scotland, Wales, and Ireland as well.

We've met wonderful people everywhere we've been. Many of them remain friends still. There is satisfaction when reading a news article about a certain area and being able to picture that town and remember.

When Bob turned eighty, having had no mishaps during those fifteen years of travel, we felt it wise to settle down, and are now living near our youngest grandchildren. We're content and busy where we are now, but wouldn't give up those years on the road for anything!

Our advice to youth: Do all that you can do—enjoy living!

—**BOB NELSEN,** born October 8, 1919, served during World War II as one of the famed Merrill's Marauders and worked in sales, and **AUDREY NELSEN,** born January 5, 1929; together raised five children.

~

I can't say much about older fiddles, but now that I've lived ninety-two years, my opinion is, old age is too high a price to pay for maturity. Still, since the only known alternatives are unacceptable, I guess the only thing left is to hang in there and do the best we can.

—**ARTIE SHAW,** born May 23, 1910, is a clarinet soloist and bandleader best known for his work during the great swing era of 1935–1945.

~

*T*urning sixty-five is one of those life passages— like college hazing and infantry basic training— many men would rather avoid contemplating until it's upon us.

At least that's the way I feel.

I suppose it's different if sixty-five means retirement, a nice pension, generous Social Security, and a move to Vero Beach. Especially if you're retiring from a job you hate. Grabbing that gold watch and peeling out of the workplace parking lot for the last time must be a fantasy right up there with winning the lottery or a hot Saturday night with Gina Lollobrigida.

Speaking for myself, I feel fortunate just to make it this far. My dad, who had looked forward to collecting Social Security from that day in 1935 President Roosevelt signed the act into law, died at sixty-four. So did his dad. Since I hit that age a year ago, I've been glancing over my shoulder more often than usual to see who or what was gaining on me.

In some societies, turning sixty-five means instant recognition for accumulated wisdom and the ability to embrace all things good and spiritual.

Oh, come on. Our culture knows better. In truth, it's more like what my best friend's dad used to tell me: "We get too soon old and too late schmart."

Sure, we've lived many of life's lessons. But they point to the past. What was important even ten years ago often isn't meaningful today. These days we don't so much fear dying as not having lived. Today any regrets are of omission.

Racing past sixty-five has little significance to me. Oh, now there's Medicare in my life. But offsetting that is the increased expense of pharmaceuticals and my sudden lack of earning power to cover their cost. (Why does our society believe that, with the blowing out of sixty-five candles, we're suddenly worth only six bucks an hour as bag boys and burger boosters?)

I'm already enjoying the perks of geezerdom. Senior discounts at the movies, that kind of thing. Since AARP now considers anyone over fifty part of the geezer gang, by the time we're sixty-five, we've been getting their discounts for a good part of our lives.

Most friends my age consider it a miracle that we've lived to this age. Says my buddy J. C. Spitznagel, "If I'd known I was going to live so long, I'd have taken better care of myself."

But even when you're fifty, you can't imagine ever being sixty-five. It simply doesn't compute.

Then, without warning, you're there. You don't feel any older. Sure, your kids are in their thirties and forties, but that's some kind of cosmic trick. You've got grandkids approaching high school but that, too, is an unexplainable aberration, a puzzling black hole in the fabric of your life.

The sad truth is, most of us are even beginning to look like we might be sixty-five. That's the tough part. Personally, I choose to ignore those telltale nose hairs, the glare of my bald spot, and my growing wattle. Not that I avoid mirrors. I simply don't recognize that fellow looking back at me.

Who is he, anyway?

I myself have a full head of hair, good looks, great muscle tone, and the flattest belly this side of the Fifth Street Gym. At least that's what I see in my mind's eye. Why that sixty-five-year-old guy in the mirror let himself go so, I have no idea. But he ought to be ashamed.

People like that give all us old coots a bad name.

—**FRANK KAISER,** born December 27, 1935, has been a writer, editor, photographer, and now writes a nationally syndicated column called "Suddenly Senior" at www.suddenlysenior.com.

∾

*W*ell, Willard, I've got to tell you that I find far too few advantages in getting old. You can't scarf food like you used to, and if you do, you pay for it. You naturally can't smoke because that will keep you from getting to 100.

But there are some positive things about aging—like not having to break your back exercising. As an older person, you can just go out, take a nice walk, maybe briskly, and everyone will agree you're doing your share—you're no slacker. Also, I've always had a tendency to be an angry loudmouth. When younger, I generally knew when to pull back in volume and anger so I wouldn't get my teeth punched out. Now as a senior citizen, I can rant and rave all I want, and I'd say no one would consider knocking me on my ass as any great achievement.

So the two big pleasures for me in aging are the slacker syndrome and the freedom to rant.

—**EDWARD ASNER,** born November 15, 1929, is an actor and played Lou Grant on *The Mary Tyler Moore Show*.

$\mathcal{J}$ ust as I seemed to be running out of "future," I discovered new wonders, new adventures, whole new worlds. Now I look back with affection on the past and forward to the future with eagerness and excitement. I joined a writing group.

Blessed with the freedom that grown kids and retirement bring, I ran down the list of all the things I wanted to do "someday." I even tried writing, but writing by myself, with no audience, was like playing the piano without a keyboard. A friend introduced me to an informal writing group.

Like high school band players who dreamed of continuing to play in a band as adults, we gather to write and share our life histories, memories, ideas, faith, and even our passions, through our writing. As we share, the barriers between us fade. We make new friends. We discover new worlds encountered by others in the group. Our writing provides the inspiration to explore life. The experience of the others reveals the means to embark on the journey.

We have no assignments. We do not criticize one another's writing. We do cheer what we find best in every piece. We have fun even though some pieces are very poignant. Many of us go to lunch together afterward. We have a good time.

We need a leader because we are an undisciplined,

sometimes rowdy, bunch. As soon as we hear a reading we really like, our minds take off and toss it about like a birdie in a mad badminton game. Our leader inhibits our exuberance without curtailing our enthusiasm so that every member who has written for the week is heard.

Our writing group is not like a class. It is not like the Internet. It is more like a band of forty musicians, of which twenty to thirty gather once a week to play. Together we turn the future into a symphony of wonder and opportunity. You could form a writing group, too, and start writing your own future.

—**NILS A. PARR**, born December 18, 1934, is a retired teacher.

∾

*O*ver the past several years my father has had quite a bit to say on the subject of aging. For instance:

"The joy is not in reaching a certain age but the fun you have on the road getting there."

"I used to say, if I had my life to live over again, I wouldn't have time. Now, I say, I wouldn't have the strength."

"The terrible thing about growing older is that it lasts so long. You start telling jokes to make a living, and one morning you wake up and find out that you've written the history of a century." (Ironically, the year 2003 is Dad's centennial year.)

On his ninety-sixth birthday, Dad pulled from his joke vault a few of his favorite jokes on the subject of growing older, and I know he would want them to be a part of Willard's book.

"Age is just a number. However, in my case it's quite a big number."

"When wine, women, and song become too much for you to handle—give up singing."

"My doctor says I have a lot going for me. Unfortunately, he can't stop any of it from going."

My mother, Dolores Hope, who is ninety-three, has a little different take on this joy of aging. A simplified statement of her philosophy is on a needlepoint pillow on her bed. It reads: "Growing old ain't for sissies."

Both my father and mother have learned not so much the secret to aging well, but the secret of living life to its fullest, sharing their life and gifts with others, and especially the joy and healing power of laughter. At their ages they are both inspirational examples of enjoying every moment of the life that has been given them.

—**LINDA HOPE** for her father, **BOB HOPE,** born May 29, 1903, and her mother, **DOLORES HOPE,** born May 27, 1909.

I'm in the Super Senior category, proudly eighty. There are various things in my life of which I'm pleased, but nothing more than this: Last May 14, I traveled solo (8,383 miles) from Maine around the U.S.A., returning home, via Canada, forty days later, June 22. It was a great experience. Not a "visiting" trip, although I did see some family and friends, it was the challenge of the *trip* itself. Something I had not done in about twenty-five years. There were no unpleasant situations; just good weather and wonderful people along the way. No, I wasn't bored. It appears that only the young get bored. There was nothing to fear, just one adventurous day after another. I love to travel and have been to all seven continents. But this spring at the winter of my life I wanted to do something special. The rewards were awesome and personal.

The other venture in my life was at age thirty-eight—I started going to college. At that time, I was a single parent, of sons eleven and twelve, working two jobs and receiving no financial assistance. I received my bachelor of arts and master of arts within ten years, attending classes evenings, Saturdays, and during summers. Only then was I able to obtain financial stability. Because of this, I have been able to

encourage several younger women to pursue their education with validity.

I strongly suggest that one should look to the future without thinking of aging. Every decade of life has its own dividend. Be a risk taker or you will spend your later years regretting things you did not do.

The great thing about getting older? My opinion is the knowledge of one's self and realization that *contentment* outlasts happiness. All in all, the *trip* is great.

—**JANET QUIRK,** born December 10, 1921, was a seamstress, occupational therapist, program analyst, assistant director for two facilities for the mentally retarded; she also worked at a school for delinquent boys, as an administrator at a school for girls, as a hearing examiner with the parole commission with the U.S. Department of Justice, and as a college instructor; she has two sons.

Cheerfulness and content are great beautifiers, and are famous preservers of youthful looks.
—CHARLES DICKENS

The best thing about growing old is having grand-children—you have all the wonderful parts of it, and they go home at night.

—DR. JOYCE BROTHERS, born September 20, 1928, is a psychologist, the writer of a daily syndicated newspaper column and several monthly magazine columns, and frequently makes film and television guest appearances.

∿

I absolutely adore being "older"! I don't have the stress of rush, rush and go, go to keep the sched-ule! I've finally come to the conclusion that it doesn't matter about a lot of things. Things I used to think were important have paled into insignifi-cance! Thank the good Lord for all of these changes. I did try to smell the flowers along the way and to pat the dog and to enjoy the sunsets, but now I *really* savor these things and additional ones besides. And, best of all, if I don't get it done today, I've come to realize, it'll still be there for me to do tomorrow! Or maybe the day after tomorrow.

—BETTY GAULT CORDOBA, born December 23, 1927, is a retired teacher and vice president of the Non-Striking Anti-Union Teachers of Los Angeles.

∿

My philosophy has become a combination of ideas from my many celebrity clients and friends, best summed up by this phrase: "You may have to get *older*, but you don't have to get *old*." I gave a psychic reading to writer W. Somerset Maugham on his eightieth birthday and I was impressed with his enthusiasm. He still had curiosity about his future. I asked what kept him young, and he said, "I've never carried the burden of memories like a suitcase on my back." I've remembered this through the years—spending too much time reliving the past, good or bad, can only weigh us down.

I, too, prefer to live for the here and now, always having a reason to get up in the morning. For me, work is the motivator. I'll never retire. I find too much pleasure in helping people, giving them psychic messages about their past, present, and future, and in contacting their loved ones on the other side.

But while I take my work seriously, I've learned not to take *myself* too seriously, and I love to smile. And if the smiles cause lines, well, I've earned them. A client and friend of mine was Adela Rogers St. Johns, the renowned journalist and White House correspondent. She once told me that friends had urged her to have some of the considerable wrinkles removed from her face. "Why?" she asked. "Each frown line . . . every smile line tells a story."

This is not to say that I'm opposed to looking one's best or taking care of oneself. But I stop short of believing in extensive plastic surgery. I've been to too many parties and seen a #2 nose or a #3 chin. Be the best "you" you can be. Play up your best features instead of trying to change what is an unattractive feature.

I try to keep a youthful glow about myself by loving life in general. And I have a "beauty" secret. Each day, whenever possible, I lie down with a chilled, herbal eye pack for less than an hour. My dear friend, singer/songwriter Anthony Newley, started me on this routine, and he used to call it a "kittywink"—shorter than a catnap. I follow this routine even when I'm traveling.

And I do love to travel, for business and pleasure. I lecture around the country and aboard cruise ships. It was on a cruise that I met a passenger who inspired me. Part of my lecture teaches people how to meditate with various colors of candles, bringing special desires into their life. There are eight colors, each representing a particular situation. When I began explaining the pink candle for career matters, asking for a volunteer to help me demonstrate, one audience member yelled out, "I'm sixty-five—I'm too old to worry about my career!" Another said, "I'm seventy and retired! I'm too old for work!"

Then, from the back of the theater, came a sprightly gray-haired man. "Kenny!" he called out. "I'll volunteer! I'm interested in work!" My volunteer, named Robert, was eighty years old. He'd had a high-level career with IBM and though he'd retired from that field, he'd had several offers for consulting work. Together, he and I worked on the visualization technique, repeated an affirmation—"Health, happiness and prosperity are meant for me; I reach out and claim them as mine"—and earned an enthusiastic round of applause.

This proves what I've always believed: Aging does not mean the end of productivity. It may instead mean freedom to explore new directions. I was shopping at a health food store one day and bumped into my friend, nutritionist Gaylord Hauser. He looked wonderful—tanned, fit, and vibrant. He enthusiastically told me his plans for the future. "Kenny," he marveled, "I'm seventy-nine years old, but my career has reinvented itself! I've hired a new agent, we're revamping my diet and nutrition advice, and reissuing my books." Gaylord remained busy until his passing some years later.

Another famous friend of mine was the legendary Mae West. Mae was a family friend and actually very psychic herself. She wrote all of her plays and screenplays while in trance, calling upon "The Forces," as she called her spirit guides. A favorite story of mine involves Mae West returning from the final day of shooting her last film, *Sextette*. She was way up in years at the time, but she'd finished the film like a trouper. She was riding silently in the back of her limousine, heading toward her home at the Ravens-wood Apartments in Hollywood. Her companion thought perhaps she was depressed about the end of filming, wondering if her life was over. But presently, Mae spoke in a strong voice, saying, "Well, that was yesterday. Now, let's think about tomorrow."

Like Mae, I try to think about tomorrow. I continue to see clients privately for psychic readings. I have two current books, *I Still Talk To . . .* and *Making Your Goals a Reality*, that keep me busy with book signings. I try to stay active as a guest on radio and television, and surprisingly I've become a favorite on many rock radio stations. It's wonderful to talk to a fourteen- or fifteen-year-old who wants a message from a loved one on the other side. Basically, the young people I've spoken to are hungry for spiritual comfort.

I credit my mother, Kaye, with two important things. She taught me about developing my psychic abilities since she, herself, was quite psychic. And she gave me my enthusiastic outlook on life. She was getting her hair and nails done right up until a few weeks before she passed. She was very conscious of her posture, never passing a mirror without looking at her reflection and straightening up.

Kaye was often mistaken for twenty years younger than her actual age. But we never discussed age—I'm not sure she even knew her real age. She'd say to me, "Don't mention age—if people will tell that, they'll tell anything personal!"

She playfully instructed me not to tell my age in public. "You'll make me seem old if you do!" she'd laugh.

I will acknowledge this much: Kaye lived a wonderfully long and happy life, passing away "somewhere in her nineties." But regarding myself, I learned my lesson from Kaye well. I won't tell my age. How do I know how old I am, really? I figure I've spent perhaps twenty-seven years sleeping—that's not really living. I've probably spent fifteen years showering and shaving—that's hardly living. I've perhaps spent nineteen years making love—now, that counts! Of course, anyone who's followed my career through the years and who knows I was psychic to Presidents Eisenhower and Truman, and the Duke and Duchess of Windsor can get a fairly good idea of my age. I started when I was a child, but still, it doesn't take a mathematical genius to figure out my age, if people are so inclined.

I would much rather remember a person's smile or something they said to me, rather than the date they said it or how old they were at the time. I leave age consciousness to others, because age can too easily become a defining factor. It becomes who we are. But who's to say what sixty-five, seventy-five, or eighty-five looks or feels like?

I gave screen legend Marlene Dietrich psychic messages on a couple of occasions, and she shared the trait of not having any concept of age. She laughingly told me about the time she returned to do a film after a lapse of many years. While watching some rough cuts of the film, she commented critically to a cameraman with whom she'd worked years before, "I don't look the same at all—you're doing something wrong." To this, the cameraman retorted, "I'm sorry, Miss Dietrich. *I'm* twenty years older!"

I refuse to let negative thinking enter my life, and repeat an affirmation: "No negative vibrations will enter today or ever." And as much as possible, I surround myself with equally positive people. My belief is that depression is a luxury very few people can afford. And jealousy is another emotion I shun. Why resent someone else's success or happiness or youth? One fact of aging that I welcome, however, is the seniors' discount. Now, that I have fun with! In many cases, you only have to own up to being fifty or fifty-five. It's more like belonging to a special discount club. What's not to enjoy about that?

Being a psychic and regularly contacting the spirit world has given me one additional blessing: I have very little fear of passing away. To me, no one *d-i-e-s,* they're only in the next room. I know that communication can still exist from one realm to the other. If we open ourselves to it, we can still feel the love from those who've passed on and vice versa. The other side is a beautiful place. Of course, I'm in no hurry to get there just yet!

—**KENNY KINGSTON** is a celebrity psychic/medium who has appeared on radio and television programs throughout the world.

∾

I must admit that when I was eighteen years old in 1945 and my aunt and uncle had their twenty-fifth wedding anniversary, I thought they looked "old" and I couldn't think of anything worse than being "old." How wrong I was!

I was married in 1948 to a wonderful man in Grand Island, Nebraska. We had a beautiful thirty-one-year marriage, until he passed away at age fifty-two. I was a widow at fifty years old with three adult sons. Fortunately, I was a professional also and continued working for seventeen years as a widow, when my "first love" found me after he became widowed. He was in Massachusetts and I was in Seattle, Washington. (We would have married when I was eighteen but my mother, a devout Irish Protestant, would not allow me to marry an Italian Catholic.) Fortunately, fate had its day and Sam found me in 1992 in Florida. He came to see me and something happened that I never dreamed could. I didn't know "old people" (ages sixty-seven and seventy-two) could be "in love." I honestly experienced all of the things young lovers do, and we were married after a short, four-month long-distance courtship. I am convinced age is a state of mind. My sons say I look younger and act younger than I did the seventeen years I was alone—and I know loving and being loved at any age is the best medicine that can be administered.

We have been married for nine years—we are seventy-five and eighty-one—and look forward to having many more happy years together. I had to replace all the pans and dishes I had given away because I was certainly never going to need any of that for entertaining, but I have a renewed interest in cooking, keeping house, and entertaining. We moved into the new house we planned and built to grow old together in; we bought pets to enjoy, and Sam said, "If we couldn't begin our life together, we will end it together." We are two very lucky people!

—LORENE M. CHIANCOLA, born November 28, 1926, was a private secretary to the mayor of her city, ran a bridal coordinating business from home, and was an assistant to a prosecuting attorney, a court reporter, and a catering sales manager.

∾

The great thing about getting older is that you can pretend you do not hear someone that you don't want to hear. Also, if you are over seventy, you don't have to do anything you don't want to do.

Television advertisers don't care about me anymore. They prefer the eighteen- to thirty-five-year-olds as customers, so I can go in and buy an automobile without anyone knowing about it.

—**ART BUCHWALD**, born October 20, 1925, is a columnist and winner of a Pulitzer Prize.

~

*B*en Franklin once said: "Most men die at thirty— they are only buried later."

Franklin's observation may be valid, but it is also true that society benefits most from those who continue to grow and contribute *after* the age of thirty. Certainly my own life has been more fulfilling since that milestone.

Ben Franklin, of all people, knew this was also a time when we can be the most valuable to our community and state, a time when we can return to society some of that which we have received from it. It is enlightened self-interest when we help make it possible for future generations to experience the same opportunities we have enjoyed.

What about those who would actually like to live right up to the time they are buried—hopefully at an advanced age? And there are far too many looking for some fountain of youth instead of embracing maturity and maximizing the satisfaction to be gained from it.

Youth and health are not simply a matter of years; they are also a state of mind. It is possible to be just as vital, just as active, just as lighthearted now as ten or twenty years ago. It is possible to cheat time, not by dwelling on diets or exercise, but through understanding of what to expect of your body today.

We are all interested in maintaining the highest quality of life in our "golden years." Experts extol the virtues of an active body and mind. That is well and good, but there is another, frequently overlooked factor that can make a contribution to enjoying our seniority—the role that risk plays in our lives.

It was risk takers who established the United States Constitution. And America was built by those who met the challenges and accepted risks, not cautious naysayers—by those who wanted to live, not simply exist. Each generation has an obligation to take some risks, to raise society to a higher plateau, to free men's minds for a look at new worlds.

We are living in the most fascinating age in history. In the 200 years since Ben Franklin shared his wisdom, Americans have had the courage and foresight to venture, not only to all corners of our world, but out into the star-studded universe itself. We are part of the generation that had the opportunity and the courage to look around the moon and reach for the stars. We did not shy from the unknown. We were willing to take a risk. Instead of waiting to be buried after the age of thirty, astronauts found it to be the most productive years of their lives.

Yes, we knew landing on the moon was a risky, dangerous adventure. But there was never any doubt that the potential gain greatly exceeded the risk. And success carried with it the promise that our children and our children's children would be exploring the frontiers of the universe. Exploration and the *chance of dangerous adventure* are basic needs of the human spirit.

The moon landing is history. In the 1960s, against enormous odds and with the whole world watching, a group of engineers, scientists, and managers accepted a challenge, took the risk, and changed the way we perceived our world. In doing so, we kept the spirit of adventure alive for one more generation.

The real payoff of Apollo was how it made us feel. It changed each and every one of us—inside. For a brief period during the time of Apollo, our society felt good about itself again; we felt together. The moon landings proudly proclaimed that we accepted no limits on what we could accomplish. We all felt alive. And it all began with a few adventurous souls willing to accept a challenge and take a risk.

Will we continue to accept challenges and take risks in the future?

Estate planning is not the only preparation when you reach "that certain age." Accepting death as an inevitable and essential part of living will remove anxiety and free you to enjoy those "golden years." The earlier in life one makes that accommodation, the better prospects for a richer life. Our presence will still be felt so long as we're remembered. For most of us, that means for our children's lives or our children's children's lives—not much more.

Today, opportunity and *the chance of dangerous adventure* have been replaced by security and a risk-free existence as the goal of most Americans. We fail today not because of our inability to do something but because of our unwillingness to tackle it in the first place. Are we doomed to a future with a fixation on safety and security, where our resources will be used only to feed our existence and never for dreaming and reaching?

If there is a purpose to man's existence, it is growth, not simply survival. Progress is made by a few individuals searching for excellence and the boundaries of our knowledge, those willing to accept a challenge and prepared to pay the price, not cautious naysayers. It's the Christopher Columbuses and the Neil Armstrongs who move us forward, not the Ralph Naders. With a Ralph Nader at the head of a wagon train, we would never have made it across the plains and over the Rockies.

There is a relationship between challenge, risk, responsibility, and leadership. Accept all the challenges you can—especially when you're young—even if it means taking some risks. Overcoming adversity instills confidence. Regardless of how long, it can be a wonderful life *if* you choose to live and not simply exist.

Don't be one of those poor, unfortunate souls who say, "If only I had my life to live over." Live your life in such a way that once is enough. Don't just take from life's experiences, give to each one—try to have a greater impact on events than they do on you. In a world that seems to go on forever, a human life is amazingly short, regardless of how long you live. Death is never very far away. It could be waiting just around the corner. If each day is filled with living, it is easy to feel "If I die tomorrow, I will die fulfilled."

There are worse things in life than dying. The joys of living are greatest for those who recognize that it's not how long you live but how you live your life that counts. Spend your life generously; don't pay it out like a miser would spend his money.

In the next century, no one will care how carefully and cautiously we survived the last quarter of the twentieth century. But they will celebrate our willingness to accept risk, to make a commitment, to expand our universe, and to change forever the way we looked at our world when we decided to land a man on the moon. You may not set foot on distant planets but you can set your mind on the future and, hopefully, return us to a society where peace, self-expression, and *the chance of dangerous adventure* are available to all.

—**WALTER CUNNINGHAM,** born March 16, 1932, was America's second civilian astronaut; he occupied the lunar module pilot seat for the eleven-day flight of *Apollo 7,* the first manned flight test of the third-generation United States spacecraft.

Afterword

*A*fter hearing what so many people with such diverse backgrounds and interests have to say on the subject of getting older, I have to agree with Donald J. Plefka: "I have a feeling of contentment and being right with the world. I do not want to be young again." And with Monty Hall—getting older *is* an honor.

I'm inspired, encouraged, and looking forward to getting older every day. I hadn't realized how much was *ahead* of me and how much more I wanted to *do*. Perhaps I'll join a singing group with Ruth B. Glass, or swim at the YMCA pool with Marilyn Tolan, or maybe hide my own Easter eggs with President Bush, or jump on board and travel the country in a motor home with Truvan T. Gibson, or call on

Helen Carlson at 2:00 P.M. to join me for breakfast, or log on and play on-line Scrabble with Tala M. Lipshutz, or give the dice a roll and join Ellamay Ciaudelli at the casinos, or perhaps join Gary Owens in a game of basketball. You can bet I'll be certain to take every opportunity to laugh like Marigrace Baldwin.

But for now I think I'll take Peter Graves up on his invitation to sit on his deck overlooking Lake Tahoe. Now *that's* certainly not a Mission: Impossible!

Index

3/12
6/6/12
7/13/14
7/25/14
6/4/16
7/3/17